A SHORT EXPOSITION

OF THE

EPISTLE TO THE GALATIANS

DESIGNED AS A TEXT-BOOK FOR CLASS-ROOM USE AND FOR PRIVATE STUDY

BY

GEORGE B. STEVENS, Ph.D., D. D.

PROFESSOR OF NEW TESTAMENT CRITICISM AND INTERPRE-
TATION IN YALE UNIVERSITY

Wipf and Stock Publishers
199 W 8th Ave, Suite 3
Eugene, OR 97401

A Short Exposition of the Epistle to the Galatians
Designed as a Text-book for Class-room Use and for Private Study
By Stevens, George B.
ISBN: 1-59752-291-0
Publication date 7/1/2005
Previously published by The Student Publishing Co., 1890

PREFACE.

THE author has aimed, in the preparation of this handbook, to supply to the student the means of clearly tracing Paul's course of thought in the Epistle to the Galatians. He has sought to present the essential results of critical study, without introducing into the exposition so many of the details of the critical process as to embarrass the mind and withdraw attention from the ideas themselves. The explanations were written with constant reference to the original text, but it accorded with the purpose which the book was designed to serve to place in connection with the exposition of each verse the translation of the Revised Version. In cases where anything could be gained for the critical student by so doing, I have placed the Greek text of the words and phrases commented upon in parenthesis. By this method I have sought to adapt the exposition alike to students of the original and of the English Version.

In a few instances it seemed necessary to comment on points connected with the original language which it was not easy to make plain to one iv *Preface.*

who should read the translation only. In such cases, I have inserted in parenthesis the English of the words in question, or, if that plan seemed unlikely to make the matter intelligible to the English reader, I have remanded the explanation to the margin. It is believed that the entire exposition, with these few exceptions, will be readily understood by the intelligent and diligent student of the English text.

Where the meaning of passages is doubtful or much disputed, I have generally mentioned in parenthesis a few prominent representatives, among well known interpreters, of the different views. It has been, however, no part of my plan to give a full account of varying interpretations; yet the brief exposition of opposing opinions in the case of obscure and difficult passages has often seemed advisable in order that the student might consider and compare the more plausible explanations.

To each chapter has been prefixed an analysis and a paraphrase. The divisions of the chapters correspond to the paragraphs in the Revised Version. To each of these I have prefixed a title which gives the leading thought of the section. These titles, taken together, constitute the analysis of the Epistle. I commend to the student the constant use of the paraphrase in connection with his effort to trace the Apostle's argument. It is often possible to bring out the essential idea of an

Preface.

obscure passage by such a free rendering more clearly than can be done by explanations in detail of the writer's own words. I have not attempted in the paraphrase to represent the minor turns and shades of thought, but rather to place in sharp relief those great central ideas, whose clear apprehension will render comparatively easy the appreciation of the more detailed explanations which are presented in the notes. It would be a great advantage for the student to read through the entire Epistle,—and more than once,—consulting the paraphrase in cases where the thought is not understood, before the study in detail is begun. By doing this, in connection with the mastery of the main points presented in the Introduction, the great advantage arising from a clear idea of the purpose and scope of the letter as a whole is gained, and the task of threading one's way through all the turnings and digressions of the thought rendered a far easier one.

The object which I have kept steadily in mind in the preparation of this manual, has been to furnish the student of the Bible,—whether a professional student of theology or not,—with an introduction to the religious and theological teaching of the Apostle Paul. The method of Biblical study, comparatively new among us, which investigates each book of the Bible, or each group of books which belong together by reason of common authorship or similarity of character, as a whole, and explains all its parts in the light of their historic occasion, purpose and peculiarities, is one of so great value and importance that it is certain to be more and more widely employed and to be adapted, in all practicable ways, to the popular study of the Bible. A wholly new light is shed upon the meaning of the Biblical books when the historic situation in which they arose is understood and their occasion and immediate purpose and use made clear.

The author's effort has been to trace the movement of the argument in this Epistle throughout in the light of those conditions which furnished the immediate occasion of its composition and did so much to determine its peculiarities. Fortunately the numerous local and personal allusions in the letter, together with kindred courses of thought in the Epistle to the Romans and historic notices in the Book of Acts, enable us to form a clear and well-defined picture alike of the condition of the Galatian churches and of the grounds of the Apostle's convictions and fears which find expression in the Epistle.

In an appendix I have presented an outline plan for the study of the Epistle which I think may be of service, especially to those who study it without the aid of an instructor. Some teachers may prefer to follow the method which is here outlined,—supplementing it perhaps, with additional material,—

Preface. vii

rather than to proceed upon the ordinary plan of studying the Epistle section by section and verse by verse. Such a course would have important advantages and could, I think, be planned with little difficulty and pursued with great profit. But whether this outline is employed in the study or not, the questions and topics which it supplies should be used in review. From them also may be derived abundant material for an examination upon the Epistle.

With these explanations of its method and purpose, the author dedicates this manual to that large and increasing company of Bible students who are eager to gain a clearer understanding and a more intelligent appreciation of the Sacred Scriptures.

YALE UNIVERSITY, October, 1890.

INTRODUCTION.

I. THE PLACE OF GALATIANS AMONG THE PAULINE EPISTLES.

GALATIANS is the earliest of the four great doctrinal Epistles of Paul (Gal., I and II Cor., Rom.). Next to Romans it is the most important for the study of the Apostle's teaching, and in the exposition of the doctrines of faith, justification and Christian freedom, is scarcely second to the longer and more comprehensive letter. It is a peculiarly desirable Epistle with which to begin the critical study of the Pauline writings, both because of its vigor, intensity and comparative brevity, and because the circumstances which called it forth were such as to lead the Apostle to concentrate his attention throughout upon the central principles of his theology and to set them in sharpest contrast with opposing principles. One who masters Galatians will the more easily master Romans; he will also find that the thoughts which are developed in this Epistle furnish, to a great extent, the key to the understanding of Paul's whole theological system.

Introduction.

II. GENERAL CHARACTER OF THE EPISTLE.

It is pre-eminently doctrinal and controversial. It most closely resembles Romans in contents ; I and II Corinthians in its mingling of doctrine and exhortation. Like Romans, it has for its central thought justification by faith. Being less systematic, however, it does not so readily admit of analysis. Romans is general, having more of the character of a treatise; Galatians is specific and is written with direct reference to local conditions. In this respect it resembles I and II Corinthians.

Our Epistle seems to have been written with the apostle's own hand (τῇ ἐμῇ χειρί, vi. 11); if so, it is the only instance (with the possible exception of the short personal letter to Philemon, see ver. 19). Paul usually dictated his letters to an amanuensis, adding with his own hand only the closing words of salutation (see notes on vi. 11).

Galatians is a peculiarly spirited, and indeed, vehement letter. It bears the clearest marks of Paul's mind and genius. Criticism has universally ascribed it to him.* Though apparently written without conscious plan, it has a striking compactness and unity. Its emphasis of faith and its bold assertions of the freedom of the Christian from the law, made it the favorite Epistle of the Reformers.

---

* The denial of its genuineness by Bruno Bauer and one or two followers, deserves mention merely as a vagary of a reckless, iconoclastic skepticism.

Luther declared: "It is my Epistle; I have betrothed myself to it."

III. ANALYSIS OF THE EPISTLE.

1. *Apologetic Section:* Chs. i. and ii.

Paul vindicates his apostolic commission and authority. His gospel was not received from men, nor from the primitive apostles even, but from heaven by direct revelation. He shows with what authority and effect he had rebuked even Peter, when, on one occasion, he had yielded too much to the extreme Pharisaic party who maintained that the Gentile converts must be circumcised and keep the law.

2. *Dogmatic Section:* Ch. iii. 1—Ch. v. 12.

In this division Paul develops the doctrine of salvation by faith alone, apart from deeds of the law. He exhibits the difference between the faith-principle and the works-principle, shows that both cannot be essential conditions of salvation and proves (chiefly from the Old Testament itself) both that faith is the only necessary condition, and that the effort to be saved by works, always has been, and always must be, futile.

3. *Hortatory or Practical Section:* Ch. v. 13—Ch. vi. 18.

This portion is occupied with warnings against the abuse of Christian freedom and the misapplication of his teaching. He exhorts the Galatians to humility and helpfulness toward the erring and reminds them of the essential Christian virtues. He closes with the assertion that the question of circumcision (on which his opponents so much insisted) is, in itself, of no importance, but that it is all-important that men should be renewed in life through Christ.

IV. THE OCCASION OF THE EPISTLE.

This occasion is found in the presence in the Galatian community of Jewish-Christian teachers who insisted that Gentiles who became Christians must also become Jews, that is, be circumcised and keep the Old Testament law as such. It is generally thought that these Judaizers had come from Palestine (so Meyer); others (as Neander) suppose that they were partly from Judea and partly native to Galatia, and still others (as Weiss) maintain that they were connected with Jewish-Christian congregations which had been gathered in Galatia previous to Paul's founding the Gentile-Christian churches in the province. No data exist for confidently settling this question. Whoever these persons were, it is certain that they did not comprehend the newness and completeness of Christianity; it was to them but an appendix or supplement to the Old Testament system. Paul was the champion of the opposite view. For him Christianity was complete in itself and those who accepted it were not under the law. His opponents' position was contrary to the decision of the Apostolic conference held at Jerusalem (Acts xv., Gal. ii.) at which the most conservative primitive apostles, Peter, James and John, had approved his teaching and disclaimed any desire to supplement or change it. (*Cf.* analysis of Ch. ii. and notes).

The Tübingen critics (Baur, Schwegler, Zeller, *et al.*) have maintained that Paul's difference was not merely with an extreme Jewish party in the church (*cf.* Acts xv. 1; Gal. ii. 12; II Cor. xi. 5, 13), but with the primitive apostles as well, and that the differences between himself and the "pillars" (Gal. ii. 9) were irreconcilable. The usual view is that there were indeed difficulties between him and them, arising out of their different circumstances and points of view, but that on full consideration, they were readily adjusted and never amounted to a fundamental opposition of opinion. The study of Ch. ii. (in connection with Acts xv.) must determine the answer to this question.

V. GALATIA AND THE GALATIAN CHURCHES.

Galatia was a province in Central Asia Minor so called from the Galli or Galatae who invaded and settled this region 280 B. C. The Roman province of Galatia, strictly speaking, included Pisidia and Lycaonia, but in the New Testament the name

Galatia is used geographically to denote the region actually occupied by the Galatian people. Ancyra was the principal city. It is a disputed point whether the Galatians were Teutons (and accordingly allied to the German peoples) or Celts (and so connected with the ancient Britons). As a representative of the former view Meyer says, "The conversion of the Galatians is the beginning of German church history."* As a defender of the latter opinion, Lightfoot declares, "They were genuine Celts belonging to the Cymric subdivision of which the Welsh are the modern representatives."† Upon the basis of this conviction Bishop Lightfoot indulges the fancy that one of these people on coming to South Britain for purposes of trade, may have planted Christianity in the British Isles. On this supposition their conversion would be the beginning of British church history.

The Galatians had become a Greek-speaking people at the time of their conversion. They were genuine Gentile-Christians and had received from the Apostle Paul himself instruction in his own type of doctrine. He twice visited them, (1) on his second missionary journey,—a fact which the Acts

---

* Introduction to Commentary on Galatians.

† Essay: "Were the Galatians Celts or Teutons?" in his Commentary on Galatians.

(xvi. 6) mentions quite incidentally. The Epistle (iv. 13, 14) supplies the additional information that he was detained among them on this visit by an infirmity which would have made him burdensome to them had they been less kind and forbearing. During this visit the churches were established (*cf.* iv. 19). (2) In the course of his third missionary journey he again visited them (two or three years after the first visit) for the purpose of strengthening and encouraging them in the Christian life (Acts xviii. 23).

Though predominantly Gentile, these churches must have had in their membership native Jews and proselytes. The Apostle presupposes their acquaintance with the Old Testament. They were affected with Jewish prejudices and were the more easily seduced into a Pharisaic interpretation of Christianity and a spirit of opposition to Paul. Moreover, they appear to have been naturally a fickle people (i. 6.; iv. 14, 15).

V. Date and Place of Writing.

A majority of scholars (chiefly on the ground of Gal. i. 6), suppose that the Epistle was written shortly after Paul's second visit during his three years' stay at Ephesus, therefore within the period A. D. 54-56. Others place it a little later during the winter which the Apostle spent at

Corinth (Acts xx. 3) and hence fix the date at A. D. 57.*

---

* It may be useful to add a grouping of the Pauline Epistles which is not only chronological but according to their subject-matter, together with their probable dates, as follows:

1. THE MISSIONARY EPISTLES (52-53).
    I and II Thessalonians.

2. THE GREAT DOCTRINAL EPISTLES (55-58).
    Galatians,
    I and II Corinthians,
    Romans.

3. THE EPISTLES OF THE IMPRISONMENT (62-63).
    Colossians,
    Philemon,
    Ephesians,
    Philippians.

4. THE PASTORAL EPISTLES (67-68).
    I Timothy,
    Titus,
    II Timothy.

ANALYSIS AND PARAPHRASE OF CHAPTER I.

1. *Salutation,* 1-5. I affirm the genuineness of my apostleship (which my opponents in Galatia have called in question) (1), and declare that I did not receive my commission from any human source, but from God, through a revelation of the risen and glorified Christ, who is the world's Saviour from sin and to whom belongs eternal glory (3-5).

2. *The truthfulness of his teaching,* 6-10. I am surprised that so soon after your conversion (or after my visit,—see notes on verse 6) you should have deserted the doctrine of grace, which I taught you, for that of works, which may be called a "different gospel," but would better (since there is but one true gospel) be called no gospel at all (6, 7). This counter-teaching only aims to mislead you and to overthrow the true Christian doctrine (7). My teaching is true and I should denounce any pretended "gospel" which was subversive of it, even though it were delivered by an angel from heaven; should any man teach contrary to my gospel of grace and faith, I pronounce a curse upon him

10 *Analysis and Paraphrase of Chapter 1.*

(8, 9). I justify this boldness and vehemence by the confident assurance that in my preaching I am not seeking human favor, but obeying God's will (10).

3. *The divine origin of his gospel,* (11–17). As a ground for my strong assertions, I allege the certainty that my teaching is not shaped by a human standard or derived from a human source, but that it came to me by a revelation of Jesus Christ (11, 12). My zealous adherence to the Jewish religion which led me to become the persecutor of the church, is proof that I could not have been transformed into a Christian Apostle by mere human means (13, 14). It was only when God, who had a great purpose to serve in my life, was pleased to reveal Christ as the truly risen and glorified Messiah to my spirit, that I became a Christian and a missionary (15, 16); after this event no more than before can my course be explained as a result of human influence or instruction (16); I did not resort (as may be supposed) to the primitive Apostles at Jerusalem, there to be taught the truths which I proclaim; on the contrary, I went away into the remote regions of Arabia whence I returned to Damascus [rather than to Jerusalem] (17).

4. *Paul's movements after his conversion* (18–24). After my conversion my course was such as to prove my independence of human teachers. For three years I did not see Jerusalem and the authorities of

the church there. At the expiration of that period, however, I went thither to interview Peter but my visit was a brief one. I only saw one other apostle (18, 19). I then returned through Syria to my native province. My brief stay in Jerusalem and Judea occasioned, indeed, a new interest and rejoicing at my conversion, but I was not there long enough so that the churches at large even knew me by sight (21-24).

THE SALUTATION : i. 1-5.

THIS is one of the briefest of the salutations to be found in the letters of Paul to the churches. The abruptness with which he plunges into the midst of his theme, and the absence of all commendation of the Galatian Christians, are noticeable features, and are doubtless explained by the Apostle's intense feeling of displeasure and grief at the readiness of the Galatians to desert the principles which he had taught them.

The passage consists of a greeting (vv. 1, 2) and, in connection with the benediction, a statement concerning Christ's saving and redeeming work. It is clear, from the parenthesis of verse 1, that Paul has the opposition to himself in the Galatian churches clearly in mind from the beginning of the letter.

1. Paul, an Apostle (not from men, neither through man, but through Jesus Christ, and God the Father, who raised him from the dead). The Apostle calls himself, as always, Paul. Why never Saul, which appears to have been his proper name? The first trace of the change of name is found in Acts xiii. 9. It is not in connection with his conversion, but directly after his separation to missionary service, that the change is found. In explanation of it various reasons are assigned:—(1) He received this new name from the converted Roman deputy, Sergius Paulus; or if he had previously received this Roman name, he began to use it in commemoration of that event (Acts xiii. 7 *seq.*); (so Meyer, Bengel and Olshausen). But there is no ground for this in the text, and it is altogether improbable that he would be named for one of his converts. (2) The Lexical meaning of "Paulus" is "small," and he so designated himself from humility (see I Cor. xv. 9); (so Augustine, Witsius). But the term "the least" (ὁ ἐλάχιστος) in that passage Paul applies to himself in view of his career as a persecutor; in other respects he maintains his full equality with the primitive Apostles, (Gal. i. ii., *passim*). (3) He had both a Jewish and a Roman name. The latter was brought into exclusive use in connection with his work as the Apostle to the Gentiles. It was either preferred by himself from a sense of fitness, or applied to him by others in recognition of the sphere of his ministry; (so, substantially, Lightfoot, Wieseler, Neander, Gloag, *et al.*). This is probably the correct view. Cf. John Mark, at first called simply John, (Acts xiii. 5), but later, as a missionary, Mark, (Acts xv. 37–39). Paul was a very common Roman name. **An apostle** (ἀπόστολος): Paul claims the same title as belonged to the twelve. Elsewhere James seems to be so entitled (i. 19).

In the connection of this very word with his name, we have the key-note of the first part of the Epistle, in which he claims the rank of an Apostle, as being equal with the twelve, and as having a direct divine commission. It is noticeable how Paul ranks himself as inferior when the faults of his life come into view (I Cor. xv. 9), but asserts his equal rank when the validity of his office is assailed.

Not from men (οὐκ ἀπ' ἀνθ.), not from men as *source;* **neither through man** (οὐδὲ δι' ἀνθ.), nor through the intervention of man as the *medium*. His apostolate is not from men, but from God as its source and authority; nor yet (οὐδέ) is it mediated through (any) man (but through Christ). God appointed him to his work; he is not a false Apostle, as the Judaizers say. Such is the force of **from** (ἀπό). He further asserts that he too (as well as the twelve) received his commission direct from Christ, and does not stand merely in the rank of such men as Timothy who were sent out by the Apostles. The suggestion of Luther and others is correct: **from** implies a contrast to "false apostles;" and **through** implies a contrast to "Christian workers who were not apostles." The change from the plural (**from men**) to the singular (**through man**) is probably made in order to adapt the expression to the coming correlative phrase, **through Jesus Christ** (διὰ Ἰησοῦ Χριστοῦ).

The exact development of the parallelism would have yielded: **Not from** (ἀπό) **men, neither through** (διά) **man, but through Jesus Christ and from** (ἀπό) **God**, where **from God** would have been correlative to **from men**, as stating the ultimate source whence his office had come. But Paul rarely carries out his parallels in so precise a manner. The mediation is here carried back and ascribed to God himself, (*cf.* Rom. xi. 36). Paul is probably thinking of the revelation made to him in the experience of his conversion as constituting his direct commission from Christ, and this, as being providential, may be said to have been given through the agency or operation of God.

God the Father (θεοῦ πατρός): the expression is closely like a proper name. God is here called Father in relation to Christ (so Meyer and Ellicott). DeWette interprets the expression as referring to God's fatherhood to all men. Usteri and Wieseler refer it to his paternal relation to Christians. Christ is named first because the statement is a climax; as if he said: "My mission is mediated through the direct call of Christ, but this call has its basis in the counsels of God himself, who was Christ's

16   *The Epistle to the Galatians.*

Father, and who was the power that wrought in and through him."

The contrast of **through man, through Christ,** would clearly indicate that Paul thought of Christ as superhuman. He was indeed a man in his manifested human life; but as the exalted partaker of the divine majesty, he was more.

Why should Paul add: **Who raised him from the dead?** How does this bear upon the assertion of his apostolic authority? He wishes to emphasize the exalted and glorious source of his calling. He is the chosen instrument of the *risen* Christ; his commission is from the God who lived behind and wrought through this earthly life of Christ; who wrought miracles through him, even the crowning miracle of raising him from the dead. It is from no less a source than this that he has derived his apostolate (so Meyer, Ellicott). The phrase ἐκ νεκρῶν **(from [the] dead)** is regularly without the article in the New Testament.

2. And all the brethren which are with me, unto the churches of Galatia:—All the brethren which are with me (οἱ σὺν ἐμοὶ πάντες ἀδελφοί), *i. e.* his traveling companions, and official assistants, such as Timothy and Titus were; *cf.* Phil. iv. 21, where from the "saints" in general, "those with him" are distinguished. It is against the Pauline usage to suppose that he means "all the Christians in the place where he wrote,"

The Salutation: i. 3.

since Paul never writes in the name of any church. **Unto the churches** (ταῖς ἐκκλησίαις): language more abrupt than is elsewhere found in the introductions to Paul's Epistles. There is no commendation of the Galatians; not even so much as would be implied in the expression "called saints," or "who are in God the Father." Clearly the Apostle has vividly and painfully in mind the extent of their apostasy, and their sad lapse from his teaching.

3. Grace to you and peace from God the Father, and our Lord Jesus Christ:—The benediction, substantially in the same form as here, is a mark of every Epistle of Paul. It is an amplification of the Jewish greeting, "Peace to thee" (שָׁלוֹם לְךָ). **Grace and peace** (χάρις καὶ εἰρήνη) are related as ground and consequence. "Grace" denotes the loving favor of God. "Peace" is the inner joy and repose of soul which follow upon it. For the Hebrew greeting of peace, see Luke x. 5, 6. **The Father** (τοῦ πατρός) here designates God as father in relation to those who send the greeting and also to the Christians addressed. **Our Lord** (κυρίου ἡμῶν): the word κύριος (Lord) came into use, perhaps, as the Greek equivalent of Rabbi (so Wieseler). It designates Christ as Master in relation to his disciples and followers; but it also goes beyond this, and designates him as the exalted One who commands his servants (δοῦλοι) and administers his kingdom on earth. Observe the conjoining of the names God and Christ by prepositions covering both names, as by **through** (διά) in the first verse, and here by **from** (ἀπό).

4. Who gave himself for our sins, that he might deliver us out of this present evil world, according to the will of our God and Father:—Who gave himself for our sins (τοῦ δόντος ἑαυτὸν περὶ τῶν ἁμαρ.): the vicarious death of Christ is here so early alluded to because the Apostle has in mind their neglect of that doctrine, (*cf.* ii. 21). Their Judaistic errors involved an abandonment of the sole saving significance of Christ's sufferings and death.*

This present evil world (ἐκ τοῦ αἰῶνος τοῦ

---

* The reading περί is best attested (*vs. Tex. Rec.* and B, ὑπέρ). The former is strictly more appropriate as applied to things; the latter as applied to persons (*cf.* I Pet. iii. 18); though Paul writes ὑπὲρ τῶν ἁμαρτιῶν in I Cor. xv. 3, and here only. With a personal noun or pronoun Paul always uses ὑπέρ in connection with the vicarious death of Christ, except in I Thess. v. 10 (and here some *MSS.* read ὑπέρ). The two prepositions are closely alike, περί meaning "on account of," "for"; ὑπέρ "on behalf of." Neither directly expresses the strict idea of vicariousness in the sense of "instead of" (ἀντί), but the context implies a vicarious self-giving. He gave himself on behalf of our sins; in order to atone for them, and to rescue us from their power. We find λύτρον ἀντὶ πολλῶν, Matt. 20. 28; also, ἀντίλυτρον ὑπὲρ πάντων, I Tim. ii. 6. We have in the New Testament no such expression as Χριστὸς ἀπέθανεν ἀντὶ ἡμῶν.

ἐνεστῶτος πονηροῦ), is the age or world-period previous to the second advent or parousia, which is evil, and is to be marked by greater wickedness as the parousia draws nigh (II Thess. ii. 3. *seq.*). The present age (ὁ νῦν αἰών, αἰὼν οὗτος) is opposed to the coming age (αἰὼν μέλλων) which ensues upon the parousia. Both are Hebraistic expressions (הָעוֹלָם הַזֶּה and הָעוֹלָם הַבָּא).

"**Present** (ἐνεστώς) **world**" (or age): Meyer renders "impending," "beginning," and understands by αἰών here, the evil period which is to immediately precede Messiah's advent. This the phrase can well mean; but the Pauline usage favors the common view, and there is no hint that the Apostle is here thinking of the "last times."*

The redemptive work of Christ is to deliver us out of the present world-age, which is evil; to take us out of relation to this evil stage of historical development, and to bring us into harmony with the principles and motives of a higher order. **Evil** (πονηροῦ) is emphatic: "evil as it is."

According to the will of our God, etc. (κατὰ τὸ θέλημα τοῦ θεοῦ) designates this self-giving and deliverance of Christ, as ordained of God. The work of Christ is an act of sovereign, divine mercy, far removed from human merit or attainment. The article of the original text which is joined to the word **God** (τοῦ θεοῦ) belongs, in my judgment, to

---

* On Paul's use of ἐνεστώς cf. Rom. viii. 38; I Cor. iii. 22.

both the word **God** and the word **Father**. The article not being necessary to the former word would hardly have been used if this meaning had not been intended (Lightfoot). It binds the two terms together, and **our** (ἡμῶν) is dependent upon both; the force of the phrase, then, is **our God and Father;** *cf.* II Cor. i. 3. Meyer and Wieseler construe **our** with **Father** only. These two constructions underlie the renderings in the Revised and the King James Versions respectively.

Many similar passages occur and the point is a doubtful one. The Greek commentators themselves differ. In saying **our** Paul is referring to the Christians. This is the prevailing New Testament usage. God is Father to his obedient sons (υἱοί). An ethical relation and harmony, and not a mere natural relation, is involved in these words. Fatherhood means more than creatorship. God is designated as Father only in relation to persons, who alone are capable of being the objects of the divine love.

5. To whom be the glory forever and ever. Amen.—The mention of God as "our Father" implies the *motif* of his will (θέλημα) in the work of Christ, viz., love, and it is this thought that calls out the ascription of praise: **To whom be the glory,** etc.

The glory (ἡ δόξα, *sc.* εἴη), means the glory which is due him for his gracious action. It is the

The Salutation: i. 5.

ascription of thankfulness and praise; the recognition of, and rejoicing in, the love and grace of God which are his peculiar glory. As opposed to this evil, passing age (aeon), Paul ascribes honor to God for "the ages of the ages;" the unnumbered, countless ages of eternity. (εἰς τοὺς αἰῶνας τῶν αἰώνων).

Amen (ἀμήν), is the Hebrew אָמֵן true, faithful; (Greek, (ἀληθινός). It is applied to God in the Old Testament. It is also used as an imprecation after prayers or oaths, Deut. xxvii. 15 *seq.*, meaning, "Surely let what has been said stand fast." In the Septuagint it is either transliterated (ἀμήν), or translated by some expression signifying "truly" or "let it be so," (as ἀληθῶς or γένοιτο). Thus it passed into the New Testament, and has become a part of the devotional language of every Christian people.

THE TRUTHFULNESS OF HIS TEACHING,
vv. 6-10.

INSTEAD of the usual thanksgiving which Paul early introduces into his letters (II Cor. is an exception), we find here an indignant rebuke for their speedy and deep fall away from the gospel which he had taught them, and their persuasion to the opinions and practices of errorists which were inconsistent with the true gospel. The Apostle adds his vehement protest against any person, be he man or angel, who may teach any other doctrine than that which he had taught them. He thus shows his profound conviction that he has taught them the truth, and that only.

6. I marvel that ye are so quickly removing from him that called you in the grace of Christ unto a different gospel:—
I marvel (θαυμάζω): Almost always after the salutation Paul continues his Epistles with an expression of thankfulness (εὐχαριστῶ); *cf.* Rom. i. 8; I Cor. i. 4. The word recalls the wonder of Jesus at the people's unbelief (Mark vi. 6, καὶ ἐθαύμασεν διὰ τὴν ἀπιστίαν αὐτῶν). **So quickly** (οὕτως ταχέως), either

The Truthfulness of his Teaching: i. 6.   23

(1), So rashly, suddenly, indicating the readiness with which they seized hold of the false doctrines (Chrysostom, De Wette); or (2), So soon after my leaving you, referring to his labors among them (Calvin, Bengel and Wieseler), or (3), So soon after their conversion. The reference to God's *calling* them favors this view (so Lightfoot, Meyer, Olshausen). **Ye are so quickly removing** (μετατίθεσθε), middle not passive (as Beza): to turn one's self from, to fall away from; so used in the Septuagint of falseness to one's allegiance. The present indicates the process as going on (*cf.* iv. 9-11). **From him that called you** (ἀπὸ τοῦ καλέσαντος ὑμᾶς), that is, God. The call of God is his gracious invitation which comes to man through the gospel. The phrase cannot refer to Paul (so Paulus) nor to Christ (so Lachmann, Calvin, Bengel). **In the grace of Christ**: The grace of Christ denotes the means by which, or, perhaps, more strictly, the sphere within which, God's call is made effectual. **Unto a different gospel** (εἰς ἕτερον εὐαγγέλιον): Thus does Paul characterize the doctrine of the Judaizers. It is, in relation to the true teaching, **different** (ἕτερον), so that the two are mutually exclusive. The Greek word here used implies a comparison between only two, one of which must be chosen. **Which is not another,** (ὃ οὐκ ἔστιν ἄλλο): The term rendered **another** (ἄλλο) implies the possession of something additional.

Their gospel would be **another,** if it added to the true; but if it took the place of the true it would be **different.** They adhere to the Jewish law in such a way as to exclude the gospel. They give up the Christian principle of grace and faith; they nullify the distinctive doctrine of Christ's redeeming death.

7. Which is not another gospel: only there are some that trouble you, and would pervert the gospel of Christ.—It was a paradox to call their doctrine a **gospel** for there can be but one. The Apostle now corrects the expression by adding: "This which I called a different gospel is no gospel at all. It is not another set along side of mine, as if there were several gospels. There can be no gospels in addition to the one." In the first phrase, **different** is the emphatic word; here it is **not. Only** (εἰ μή; lit. "except"). Their doctrine can be called **another gospel** only in the sense that it is a perversion of the true. This again is a modification of the correction made in the expression: **which is not another.** The sense is: "Theirs is a different gospel, that is, no true gospel at all, but only a perversion of the gospel."

There are some that trouble you (ταράσσοντες): This verb is often used of throwing into doctrinal unrest, by unsettling the mind (Acts xv. 24). The force of **would pervert,**

($\theta \acute{\epsilon} \lambda o \nu \tau \epsilon \varsigma$ $\mu \epsilon \tau a \sigma \tau$. lit., "wish to pervert") can hardly be, (as Bengel), "wishing, but not able to pervert," for they certainly accomplished their object; but rather, "they are those who will to do it, who have this purpose." *Cf.* "If any man wills ($\theta \acute{\epsilon} \lambda \epsilon \iota$) to do his will," etc., John vii. 17.

Pervert ($\mu \epsilon \tau a \sigma \tau \rho \acute{\epsilon} \psi a \iota$), means to distort a thing, so that it is no longer its true self. What Paul meant can be seen from iii. 3. From a doctrine in the sphere of the Spirit, they now departed to one in the sphere of the flesh, placing salvation in meritorious outward acts and observances, by adherence to Jewish law. **Gospel of Christ:** The phrase **of Christ** ($X \rho \iota \sigma \tau o \widetilde{\upsilon}$) is probably objective genitive, designating Christ as the theme and content of the gospel, as commonly in the New Testament where this phrase is used, and this was the gospel which Paul had preached to them. Paul maintains the identity of "his gospel" with the gospel which was related to, and connected with Christ, as opposed to all doctrines of Jewish legalism and meritorious obedience.

8. But though we, or an angel from heaven, should preach unto you any gospel other than that which we preached unto you, let him be anathema:—But though we ($\grave{a} \lambda \lambda \grave{a}$ $\kappa a \grave{\iota}$ $\grave{\epsilon} \grave{a} \nu$ $\dot{\eta} \mu \epsilon \widetilde{\iota} \varsigma$): The strict sense of this expression is "even if," rather than "although" ($\grave{\epsilon} \grave{a} \nu$ $\kappa a \acute{\iota}$), and indicates an extremely improbable supposition. "Even if we" (the Apostle and his fellow laborers, i. 2) or, indeed, an angel from heaven, etc. It is doubtful if Paul ever uses **we** (ἡμεῖς) to denote merely himself as an individual. **Other than that which** (παρ' ὅ): The relative pronoun (ὅ) can refer to the word **gospel** (εὐαγ.), "to that gospel which," or be general, "to what" we have preached (Meyer). The preposition here used (παρά) implies a comparison of the two in which they exclude one another: If any one preaches a **different gospel,** one which is contrary to, or inconsistent with ours, etc. In former times there was a doctrinal controversy connected with this word between Lutherans and Roman Catholics regarding tradition. Was it said only that what is *contrary* to the gospel is accursed (the R. C. view); or that what is additional to, supplementary of it, is also condemned (Lutherans)? *i. e.* Is supplementary tradition allowable or not?

Let him be anathema (ἀνάθεμα ἔστω): The word **anathema** denotes a thing devoted to God; either in the sense of an offering, gift, etc. (Luke xxi. 5, so only here in the N. T.), or as consigned to divine punishment *i. e.;* devoted to destruction, (so in six New Testament passages.)* *Cf.* our English

---

* It is the Septuagint word for the Hebrew חֵרֶם which has the same twofold signification, in accordance with the use of the Hiphil of חרם, "to devote," (*cf.* for example, Lev. xxvii. 28, with Deut. ii. 34). In the latter meaning it is something worthy or destined to be destroyed utterly.

The Truthfulness of his Teaching: i. 9.

"devote" and Latin *sacrare*. In later times this word, and the verb "to anathematize" (ἀναθεματίζειν), were applied to Ecclesiastical censures and excommunication. This force of the terms is not found in the New Testament. Anathema here means "an accursed thing." Luther renders: *der sei verflucht. Cf.* Gal. v. 10.

9. As we have said before, so say I now again, If any man preacheth unto you any gospel other than that which ye received, let him be anathema.—This phrase **As we have said before** (ὡς προειρήκαμεν) may either refer to v. 8 (so the older interpreters, Reformers, and Neander), or to what he had said when he was among them, (probably on his second visit (Acts xviii. 23); (so Ellicott, Lightfoot, Meyer, Wieseler). No grammatical reasons are decisive, but it is more natural to suppose that **So say I now again** (καὶ ἄρτι πάλιν λέγω) refers to something past, a previous occasion, rather than to what he has just written.*

10. For am I now persuading men, or God? or am I seeking to please men? if I were still pleasing men, I should not be a servant of Christ:—For am I now persuading, etc. Explanation of his boldness

---

* The student of the original text will note the unclassical use of the accusative (ὑμᾶς) for the dative after εὐαγγελίζομαι.

and vehemence. **For** (γάρ) gives the ground or reason for his daring assertion. The truth of the second alternative implied in his question is the ground of his boldness. "Am I engaged in an effort to please men, or is this a case of fealty to God? It is the latter, hence I must proclaim and defend my doctrine which conserves the truth and the honor of Christ." The word **persuade** (πείθω) is used here in a frequent classical sense, "conciliate," "win favor with," cf. Acts xii. 20 (πείσαντες Βλάστον). The **now** (ἄρτι) may imply a contradiction to the alleged occasions on which the Judaizers say he acted as a Jew (Lightfoot); or may refer to the time of his conversion (Wieseler); but probably rather serves to emphasize the present critical moment (Meyer). "Now of all other times am I seeking the favor of men?" etc.

Or am I seeking (ἢ ζητῶ): The same thought is taken up in a more general form. It is a question as between pleasing men or God. Paul cannot yield here without "obeying men rather than God." **If I were still** (ἔτι): If I yet, since my conversion (Wieseler), or, if I am still, as you say, a man-pleaser, preaching circumcision when occasion demands (cf. v. 11). **A servant of Christ** (Χριστοῦ δοῦλος): The expression refers to his *moral* relation to Christ, Christ's true and faithful bondman (Meyer, Wieseler), and not to a *historical* relation (Chrysostom, Schott, Rückert), as if he said: "If I were now pleasing men I should have remained a Pharisee and a persecutor and never have become a Christian and an Apostle." Meyer regards **servant** here as an unofficial, Wieseler as the official title of his apostleship.

THE DIVINE ORIGIN OF HIS GOSPEL,
vv. 11-17.

VERSES 11, 12 bring forward the main theme of the Apologetic Section, the Independence and Divine Origin of his Gospel. After the impassioned outburst of feeling in verses 6-10, the Epistle continues in a calmer strain, and with a certain solemnity.

11. For I make known to you, brethren, as touching the gospel which was preached by me, that it is not after man. —**For I make known,** etc. (γνωρίζω γὰρ ὑμῖν); **I make known** (γνωρίζω) introduces a formal and solemn declaration. It was indeed known to them before, but not appreciated. "I make you aware; I would impress it upon you." So in I Cor. xv. 1; II Cor. viii. 1. "I urge again upon your attention, and for your reception, the same doctrine which I formerly preached to you; and as connected with this doctrine, the specific thing which I urge is, that it is not a human work but a divine." **Brethren** (ἀδελφοί) indicates a changed phase of the Apostle's temper. He had reproached them; he will

The Divine Origin of his Gospel: i. 12

now reason with them, and win them. **The Gospel** (τὸ εὐαγγέλιον) is used by attraction or anticipation, as the object of **I make known,** with which the sentence beginning with **that** (ὅτι) is in grammatical apposition. The other construction would have been: **I make known to you that the gospel which was preached by me is not after man** (γν. ὅτι τὸ εὐαγ. τὸ εὐαγ. ὑπ' ἐμοῦ ἐστιν κ. τ. λ.); or: **I make known to you concerning the gospel which was preached by me, that it is not after man** (γν. ὑμῖν περὶ τοῦ εὐαγ. τοῦ εὐαγγελίσθεντος ὑπ' ἐμοῦ ὅτι κ. τ. λ.).—**Not after man** (οὐ κατὰ ἀνθ.=κατὰ θεόν) designates not only its origin as not human but its character as well. It was not a human work or product.

12. For neither did I receive it from man, nor was I taught it, but it came to me through revelation of Jesus Christ. This verse contains the proof of the statement immediately preceding. **For neither did I** (οὐδὲ γὰρ ἐγὼ παρὰ ἀνθρώπου παρέλαβον αὐτό): The use of the pronoun (ἐγώ), so commonly omitted, seems to show that the word **neither** (οὐδέ) has its proper adversative force: neither did I *any more than the original twelve,* etc. Since Paul so frequently compares himself with the twelve in relation to his authority and the validity of his apostolic call, it is natural to think that this thought is here in mind. (So Meyer, Wieseler, Ellicott, Olshausen). Others (as

Lightfoot) make the word **neither** simply continuative, and do not find the force of an implied comparison in the **I** (ἐγώ). **Neither did I receive it,** states the general fact that his gospel was not communicated to him from a man, but from Christ. **Nor was I taught it** (οὔτε ἐδιδάχθην) denies more specifically that it is the result of his own study under any one's instruction. The contrast to this statement is found in **through revelation** (δι' ἀποκαλύψεως). **Of Jesus Christ** (Ἰησοῦ Χρ.) is the genitive of the subject, **revelation from Jesus Christ.** The context only decides the sense of this phrase since it occurs in both the subjective and the objective force. The point is, "My doctrine is not a matter of instruction, but of revelation; not a human product, but a divine."

The passage suggests such inquiries as: What was this **revelation** and when did Paul receive it? Does he mean to say that every doctrine and opinion which he taught was a matter of supernatural revelation; or would the supposition that he received the central principles of his doctrine thus, and developed and applied them by reflection and reasoning, satisfy his language, and accord with the facts? How much does he mean to embrace in that **gospel** which he declares to have been a matter of revelation? *Cf.* on these points his other claims as a recipient of revelation. Eph. iii. 3; II Cor. xii. 1; Acts xxii. 17, *seq.*

As to the reference in the word **revelation,** the following opinions are current: (1) The revelations mentioned in II Cor. xii. 1. (2) Revelations from Christ in general. (3) A special revelation received not long after his conversion, on his way to Damascus (so Meyer and apparently Ellicott). (4) A revelation in connection with his experience on the way to Damascus (so Wieseler, Usteri, Rückert, Olshausen). Either (3) or (4) is to be preferred. It is not possible to decide confidently between them. The revelation (see ver. 16) was such a manifestation of Christ to the Apostle's soul that he saw him in his true character as the Saviour,—a revelation which destroyed forever his Pharisaic theories and gave him a new principle of religion. The reference in vv. 13-16 to his conversion makes it necessary to assume that the revelation was closely connected with the experience of his conversion. The whole drift of the Epistle shows that by his **gospel** he is thinking of those distinctive principles which he opposed to the Judaizing errors,—grace, faith, and Christ as sole Saviour. It is against the facts to suppose that Paul claimed a direct supernatural attestation of his every argument or opinion. See I Cor. vii. 12, 25, 26. It was those central principles which made the gospel what it was, and which, if overthrown, nullified its character, that Paul had received as divine, and for which he claimed the direct authentication of Christ.

We cannot suppose that Paul knew nothing of Christian doctrine before this revelation. The point is, that no such knowledge convinced him, or made the gospel *his* gospel. It was in the crisis when Christ stood revealed to him and in him (ἐν ἐμοί, ver. 16), that he received the divine authentication; so that his certainty rests on no reasoning or argument, but on a divine revelation. The vision of Christ, the revelation of Christ to him, convinced him of what he had often heard, that Christ was the Son of God. This new conviction carried everything with it. If he was the Messiah, then he did not die for his own sins, but for others'. His death must therefore be the means of salvation. He is the suffering Messiah of Old Testament prophecy (I Cor. xv. 3, 4). He is the bringer of God's grace to men, and the way to God is through faith in him. Thus Paul's gospel springs directly from the certainty given in the revelation that Christ is the true Messiah, the Son of God. Accordingly, the first assertion that he made as a Christian was that "Jesus is the Son of God." (Acts ix. 20.)

Having asserted (vv. 11, 12) his apostolic authority, and the independence of his doctrine, the Apostle now enters upon a detailed proof of his statement (vv. 13-24). In addition to the general analysis already given the points of this proof may be stated more in detail, thus:—

The Divine Origin of his Gospel: i. 13.

(1). My career (ἀναστροφή) as a strict Jew and persecutor of Christianity proves that no mere human persuasion could have transformed me into an Apostle, v. 13.

(2). My intense prejudice and attachment to Jewish traditions, rendered me impervious to mere human influences, v. 14.

(3). I did not communicate or consult with men about the change, vv. 15, 16.

(4). I did not confer with the prior Apostles. I kept aloof from Jerusalem, the seat of apostolic authority. I withdrew into retirement, v. 17.

(5). When later I visited Peter, I saw but one other Apostle, v. 19.

(6). The people of Judea did not even know me by sight; they had merely heard of my conversion and rejoiced in it, but that was all. I could not, therefore, have been under instruction at the center of apostolic teaching and influence. My relations and history do not permit the supposition that I received my gospel from any human source, 22–24.

13. For ye have heard of my manner of life in time past in the Jews' religion, how that beyond measure I persecuted the church of God, and made havoc of it:— **For ye have heard** (ἠκούσατε): emphatically prefixed. My course of life was something notorious and requiring no proof. **My manner of life,** way of acting, uniformly rendered "conversation" in A. V. (so in 13 passages). This translation was not incorrect when made, but owing to the change of meaning which "conversation" has undergone, does not convey the true idea. We have here a later usage of the Greek word (ἀναστροφή), which in the classical language means a "turning about" (as in battle) or a "dwelling." **In time past** etc., a designation of the time when he was living in the condition and under the prejudices of a Jew. **Beyond measure** (καθ' ὑπερβολήν), literally, "in accordance with excess." **I persecuted and made havoc** (ἐδίωκον, ἐπόρθουν): The imperfect tenses denote the course of conduct in which he was continuously engaged. The verb uniformly translated **made havoc** in the R. V., is used in application either to the organization, the church, or to the people composing it. It means more than to disturb and break up the organization. Saul killed as well as disturbed. *Cf.* Acts xxii. 4.

14. And I advanced in the Jews' religion beyond many of mine own age among my countrymen, being more exceedingly zealous for the traditions of my fathers:— **I advanced,** etc., (προέκοπτον): The word literally means "to strike forward," and so to advance, and is applied to time or to growth in character, in the New Testament. The meaning is:—"I advanced in that mode and sphere of life in which I formerly acted." *Cf.* Acts xxii. 3. **Many of mine own**

age, compeers, companions. **Among my countrymen,** (ἐν τῷ γένει μου), literally, "in my race." The term for "race" (γένος) may be used of communities larger or smaller, ranging from the family to the nation; here, probably, it denotes the Jewish people.

Being more exceedingly zealous, etc., (περισσοτέρως ζηλωτὴς ὑπάρχων): This is said with reference to the preceding **many,** "being in a higher degree than the many a zealot." **For the traditions,** etc.: The genitive here (παραδόσεων) is the genitive of the object, denoting the matters with which the zeal occupied itself. These were the Pharisaic traditions relating to Scripture, fine distinctions in conduct, principle, etc., which we meet with in the Gospels. In designating them as his own (μου), he no doubt refers to those specific traditions which characterized his party, the Pharisees. In using the term "zealot," it is not probable that he means to say that he belonged to the faction of the Pharisees which took this name in the later Jewish times, and to which belonged the apostle Simon "the Cananean" (that is, the "zealous," קַנָּא), Mk. iii. 18, —or "the Zealot," Luke vi. 15. Such had been his former life. How unlikely from a human point of view, that he ever should become an Apostle or a Christian. No mere human means could have effected it. When therefore his conversion came, it was a work of God's sovereign grace.

15. But when it was the good pleasure of God, who separated me, even from my mother's womb, and called me through his grace.—This work Paul grounds in the purpose of God, which here is not, as so often, referred to eternity, but is traced back only to the time of his birth. What God has done, he from the beginning of his life intended to do. **But when** (ὅτε): when the set time of the divine counsel arrived. The order of thought is, (1) God determines (ὁ ἀφορίσας) upon him as an Apostle from the time of his birth. (2) The call (καλέσας) comes to him,—referring to the experience on the way to Damascus. (3) The revelation (ἀποκαλύψαι) follows,—referring either to the experience of his conversion, or to experiences in close connection with it. Thus again it is shown how independent of men his apostleship was. He had it as the result of a divine decree and call, and through a revelation. When this divine work had been wrought he followed in the line of its indications. He did not proceed to fall back upon human authority and guidance, as might be supposed.

16. To reveal his Son in me, that I might preach him among the Gentiles; immediately I conferred not with flesh and blood:—In me (ἐν ἐμοί) is variously interpreted: (1) instrumentally, "by means of me" (to others), so Lightfoot, on the ground that this makes a third and distinct point in the actions of vv. 15 and 16. (2) In my soul, or in my consciousness (Ellicott, Meyer), denoting such a disclosure of Christ to the Apostle, that he became known to Paul as his own and the world's Saviour. The latter view is preferable, because (*a*) this is the natural force of the preposition used (ἐν); (*b*) the Apostle's experience, the making effectual of the divine call, would naturally be the next step of thought, rather than the work of Paul as an Apostle. He is dealing with what happened at the outset of his Christian life. This is the "revelation" (*cf.* v. 12) in which Paul received his "gospel." What may have been the time, method, or accompaniments, we do not precisely know; these are subordinate questions. The revelation gave him that knowledge of Christ as Messiah and Saviour compared with which he counted all other things as worthless (Phil. iii. 8). The time came when he saw Christ in his true glory and saving power. In that vision of the soul, all things were changed. He saw his former folly and wickedness; the path of meritorious performance closed before him, and that of faith opened. Henceforth he seizes the principles which became central for all his later teaching; he has his gospel of grace and faith. In the revelation was contained his mission. When Paul saw that Christ was Messiah and Saviour, he saw that all narrowness and Jewish legalism must disappear; that Christ was the head of a kingdom which was to be universal. It was his duty to promote this kingdom as eagerly as he had tried to promote the legal system. **Immediately I conferred not** (εὐθέως οὐ προσανεθέμην κ. τ. λ.): The word **immediately** belongs to the four verbs following (two negative and two positive), and shows the course which he forthwith pursued; *i. e.* directly after his conversion and the revelation of Christ to him; there was no interval during which human means could have taught him the gospel. **I conferred not,** "did not apply to" "consult." **Flesh and blood** (בָּשָׂר וְדָם) is the Hebrew idiom for man,—mankind. It is several times used in the New Testament, denoting either the grossness of the corporeal nature (I Cor. xv. 50) or man in his incompetence as opposed to God, (Matt. xvi. 17).

17. Neither went I up to Jerusalem to them which were apostles before me: but I went away into Arabia; and again I returned unto Damascus:—Neither went I up (οὐδὲ ἀνῆλθον): He did not resort to the great seat of apostolic influence, Jerusalem. The reference in the statement, **I went away,** is to Damascus. That he should go to Jerusalem might have been expected. Three years intervened, however, before he visited Jerusalem at all after his conversion. He designates the twelve as "those who were apostles before me," thus claiming that priority of time was the only mark of superiority belonging to their office as compared with his. After the sojourn in Arabia, he returned to Damascus, where he has a perilous experience in being let down along side the city-wall in a basket. (Acts ix. 24 *seq.*; II Cor. xi. 32 *seq.*) Where Paul sojourned in Arabia is unknown, whether in the Sinaitic peninsula or in some region not far from Damascus. Arabia was a vague term which might include regions so distant. Luke does not mention this sojourn, and seems to have had only an indistinct knowledge of the chronology of Paul's life in the years directly following his conversion, as he calls the period between his conversion and his visit to Jerusalem "certain days" ($\dot{\eta}\mu\acute{\epsilon}\rho\alpha\iota$ $\iota\kappa\alpha\nu\alpha\acute{\iota}$),—Acts ix. 23,—an expression which he could hardly have used had he known of this sojourn, and that the "considerable number of days" were three years. Nor do we know the length of time which this sojourn covered. It is not certain that it occupied the entire three years. Nor do we know its purpose. The patristic view was that he went into Arabia to preach. The modern conjecture is, that he went for meditation, study and thought, as a preparation for his public life.

18. Then after three years I went up to Jerusalem to visit Cephas, and tarried with him fifteen days.—This visit is, no doubt, identical with that related in Acts ix. 26–30. The only objection to this identification is found in the differences between the two narratives; but we have already seen that Luke's information concerning this period must have been scanty; and it is not strange that, writing from a different point of view, his account has few points of contact with Paul's own, given for a special purpose.

In Acts are mentioned the following particulars: (*a*) Suspicion of Paul on the part of the Jerusalem Christians. (*b*) Barnabas introduces him to the Apostles, and explains his conversion and preaching at Damascus. (*c*) Paul preached repeatedly in and about Jerusalem, especially to the Hellenists. Paul's own account makes no allusion to (*a*), nor to (*b*), and states that he saw but two Apostles, Peter and James. Luke evidently supposed him to have been introduced to the whole company. It is possible to explain this seeming difference by saying that all were absent from Jerusalem except Peter and James. Paul's mention of two Apostles only is not a contradiction to the inexact expression "the apostles," (Acts ix. 27), although the two narratives, independently considered, would produce different impressions. Luke's description of his preaching in and about Jerusalem gives a different impression from Paul's statement that he was unknown by sight to the people of Judea. Luke however mentions that his preaching was to a certain class, the Greek-speaking Jews. **After three years,** doubtless reckoned from his conversion, and not from his return from Arabia, since the former is the great event from which the narrative proceeds. **To visit** (ἱστορῆσαι) **Cephas:** The word rendered **to visit** is thought to be allied to the words meaning to see, and to know (ἰδεῖν, οἶδα) and therefore means, primarily, to look into, and so to examine, search; whence our English word "History." In later Greek it is used of seeing in the sense of making the acquaintance of and occurs only here in the N. T. The Aramaic name **Cephas** is supported by some of the most important authorities as against the majority of MSS., and is confirmed by ii. 9-11. This name was still, no doubt, in familiar use. Paul's purpose to make Peter's acquaintance confirms the fact, which is otherwise attested, that he had a certain precedence. Paul no doubt states the duration of his stay, **fifteen days**, as showing that so short a sojourn could not have been intended or have served for receiving instruction in the gospel. Both the purpose and the duration of the visit would tend to establish this conclusion. According to Luke (Acts ix. 29), he left Jerusalem because of plots against his life.

19. But other of the apostles saw I none, save James the Lord's brother.—Another fact bears in the same direction. He saw only one other Apostle, **James the Lord's brother.** This is the man who is later called Bishop of Jerusalem; the James who appears at the first apostolic council (Acts xv.), the writer of the Epistle, and the proper brother of Jesus.* The question arises, Is James here called an apostle? *i. e.* does (1) the word **Save** (εἰ μή) bear as an exception against **I saw** (εἶδον) only, (I saw no other Apostle; I saw only James)? (so Fritzsche, Winer, Wieseler), or (2) against the whole previous sentence (I saw no other of the Apostles, except that I saw James)? (So Meyer, Lightfoot and Ellicott). *Cf.* I Cor. xv. 7, where James is clearly spoken of as an Apostle, though distinguished from the twelve. That he saw but these two would increase the improbability that he learned his gospel at Jerusalem.

20. Now touching the things which I write unto you, behold, before God, I lie not.—The aspersions of his enemies lead him to solemnly assert that in narrating these circumstances so directly bearing upon the independence and validity of his apostleship, he speaks the exact truth. The verse is loosely constructed. A literal translation would be: "But what things I write to you, behold before God that I do not lie." The sentence "that I do not," etc., can either be understood as an anacoluthon depending on **I write** (γράφω) repeated (so Meyer); or one may suppose that there is implied in the words **before God** some

---

* See Lightfoot's Dissertation: "The Brethren of the Lord" in his Commentary on Galatians.

such thought as: "I call you to witness" (that) etc. (So Lightfoot and Wieseler). Others (as Ellicott and De Wette) supply such a thought as: "I assert," "I solemnly declare" from the context. This seems the most natural explanation since with such expressions as **before God** some such word is generally used by Paul, and the thought of it is implied here, leaving the verse a graphic anacoluthon. The R. V. omits the translation of (ὅτι) ("that").

21. Then I came into the regions of Syria and Cilicia.—Luke says (ix. 30) that Paul went from Jerusalem to Caesarea and Tarsus. Paul's explanations are general, the design being to show that he went to regions remote from Jerusalem. The two accounts coincide in that Tarsus was a city of Cilicia, and they in no respect conflict. The data are not sufficient to determine the order of his movements.

This Caesarea is probably the Roman capital of Judea. From Caesarea he could travel either by land (Meyer) to Syria, (whose capital was Antioch), and to Cilicia in the northwest, or (Lightfoot) could go by sea.

22. And I was still unknown by face unto the churches of Judea which were in Christ:—And I was still unknown: That he should be unknown to the churches of Judea is not inconsistent with his preaching in and around Jerusalem (narrated by Luke, Acts ix. 28 *seq.*) especially since he labored there distinctively among the Hellenists. To the great mass of Judean Christians he must have been unknown except by report. If, on the contrary, he had been a pupil of the Apostles he would naturally have associated with the Judean Christians.

23. But they only heard say, He that once persecuted us now preacheth the faith of which he once made havoc.—The force of the expression **the faith** here approaches the later doctrinal usage. He preached the doctrine of the necessity of faith in Christ; meaning, however, not primarily a certain doctrine about Christ, but personal belief on Christ. **Faith** always means personal faith in Christ in the New Testament (even in Acts vi. 7) but, as Meyer says, it may be objectively considered; *i. e.*, regarded as a principle governing conduct, requiring defense, etc., (Jude 3). To preach the faith is the same as to preach the gospel which required faith. So Wieseler, Meyer, Dwight (notes in Meyer's Commentary on Romans i. 5) Ellicott. *Per contra*, Thayer's Lexicon, Lightfoot (Com. p. 157), Pfleiderer.

24. And they glorified God in me:—In me, *i. e.*, "in my case." They considered Paul's conversion as an occasion and ground for rendering praise to God. There could then have been no such opposition between his gospel and that of the other Apostles as the Tübingen critics maintain.

ANALYSIS AND PARAPHRASE OF CHAPTER II.

1. *The approval of Paul's Gospel by the Primitive Apostles*, vv. 1-10.—It was fourteen years before I again visited Jerusalem; when I did so it was in response to an impulse from the Spirit and with the desire to be assured by the Apostles there in person that my teaching was acceptable to them (1, 2). So far from their criticising or amending my teaching they did not even require the circumcision of my Gentile traveling companion, Titus, (though in the circumstances to do this might have been natural and, in itself, allowable); there were, indeed, those who urged it but I refused to allow it because of the presence of Pharisaic extremists who, by insisting upon the necessity of circumcision in order to the attainment of salvation, sought to restrict our freedom as Christians from the law, and to put us again under its burdens; to have yielded would, in this case, have compromised the essential principles of the gospel, (3-5). [Verses 5 and 6 are a digression treating of the attitude of the extreme Jewish party, as contrasted with the Apostles; at

verse 6 the thread which was dropped for a moment at the end of verse 3 is resumed]. The influential primitive Apostles [and however great their influence or authority might be, it could not affect the truth and divineness of my mission, since God's approval does not follow human judgment], did not in any way attempt to supplement or correct my teaching, but rather agreed that I had as truly a divine commission to continue my present work among the Gentiles as Peter to proceed with his among the Jews (6, 7); this conviction was based upon our success in our respective spheres of labor (8). The three who were present at this interview accordingly approved the course and teaching of myself and Barnabas, and in token of this approval gave us the right hand of fellowship and commended us in our Gentile-Christian mission (9), only urging us to continue mindful of the poor Christians at Jerusalem, and to collect from the wealthier Gentile churches contributions to their support, thus keeping this bond of Christian charity between the Jewish and Gentile Christians and, by so doing, helping to prevent jealousy and alienation (10).

2. *Peter's inconsistent action at Antioch and Paul's reproof of his course,* vv. 11–21.—On a later occasion at Antioch I equally maintained my independence. Peter had been accustomed, when there, to mingle freely with the Gentile converts who had not been circumcised (*cf.* vv. 7–9), eating at the

Analysis and Paraphrase of Chapter II. 49

same table with them at the love-feasts. But certain Judaizers, alleging the authority of James for their position (see notes on ver. 12), had opposed this fellowship with the uncircumcised, and Peter, on this occasion, timidly yielded to this persuasion and withdrew from the company. For this I rebuked him because he was worthy of blame (11, 12). The other Jewish Christians followed his example, not excepting my companion Barnabas (13). Deeply feeling that the integrity and sole sufficiency of the gospel was compromised by this action, I publicly challenged Peter in the matter as follows: How is it that you now deviate from your ordinary and normal course of freely associating with Gentile converts and not only renounce that course but go farther and by your action demand that even Gentiles shall live as do the Jews, that is, be circumcised and observe the law (14)? We Jewish Christians have long ago learned that it is faith in Christ, not works of law, which saves us. How is it, then, that you now act as if legal observance was also necessary, thus inconsistently, by your action, denying that the faith which we hold is sufficient (15, 16)? If now we again resort to the legal course may it not give occasion to say that we confess ourselves still unforgiven sinners and that Christ, so far from delivering us from sin and its curse, plunges us deeper into it? We cannot admit any such conclusion and no more can we tolerate any principle of action that (like yours in this case) gives occasion to it. The real "transgressor," the "sinner," is not the man who renounces the law altogether and clings solely to Christ (as we all should), but it is he who tries to "build up again those things which he destroyed," that is, to still cling to and even to insist upon the observance of the legal system whose renunciation as a means of salvation is logically involved in the very idea of Christian faith, which means the sole sufficiency and necessity of Christ. Hence it is the Judaizing course, rather than that of the Gentile Christians, which stamps those who pursue it as "sinners"—unjustified persons, by the tacit confession contained in the idea that something additional to faith in Christ is needful (17, 18). For the law itself through its revelation of my sin to me and its ethical death-sentence, slew me. I thus broke all relation to the law, as earthly relations are broken by death (19). I died to the old life and old relations with Christ on the cross, and yet, in a new and higher sense, I live; or rather, it would be more correct to say, that Christ lives in me, for my new spiritual life has its source and support in him, who, through love, gave himself up to death for my salvation (20). My doctrine, thus, magnifies God's grace (as is not the case with those who still cling to the law and to works), and well I may, for if men could ever have been justified by the law, Christ need not have died;

Analysis and Paraphrase of Chapter II.

and, since it is an axiom with all Christians that Christ's death was not for naught, that fact may prove the entire futility of seeking righteousness in any other way than through faith in him (21).

CHAPTER II.

I. THE APPROVAL OF PAUL'S GOSPEL BY THE PRIMITIVE APOSTLES, 1-10.

ON another visit to Jerusalem he had laid his gospel before the chief authorities there, and they had approved him as a divinely sent Apostle.

1. Then after the space of fourteen years I went up again to Jerusalem with Barnabas, taking Titus also with me:— **Then** might refer either to the journey to Syria and Cilicia (Meyer), or to his first journey to Jerusalem (Wieseler). **After the space of** (διά), literally, "through." This temporal use of the preposition results from the conception of traversing the time. Should the fourteen years be reckoned from his conversion (Wieseler, Ellicott), or from the first visit to Jerusalem (i. 18), (Meyer, Lightfoot)? The word **again** (πάλιν) favors the latter view. This is the journey related in Acts xv., and the third visit of Paul to Jerusalem. For the view that it was the second, see Meyer on the passage, who maintains that Paul could not have omitted the mention of a journey to Jerusalem here without breaking down his argument. Therefore the narrative of the journey in Acts xi. 30 and xii. 25 is, in his opinion, only semi-historical. Paul turned back before reaching Jerusalem. Gal. ii. synchronizes therefore with Acts xv.; but that is the second, not the third journey as Luke would make it.

The second visit (Acts xi. 27–30) was for a special purpose, viz., the carrying of a gift of alms to the poor and persecuted at Jerusalem, and Paul has no occasion to mention it here. This then is that visit during which he attended the apostolic council.*

The following differences between the narratives in Acts xv. and Gal. ii. may be noted:—

(*a*) Acts xv. 2 states that Paul and Barnabas were sent by the church of Antioch to Jerusalem; Gal. ii. 2 makes him to go in consequence of a special revelation. But this representation is not inconsistent with Luke, who states the historical and human side, while Paul, with his special purpose in mind, states the providential side of the event.

(*b*) Acts xv. 4–7, describes a general council; Gal. ii. 2, speaks only of a private interview with the influential Apostles. Luke's narrative is general,

---

* For the discussion of the relation of Acts and Galatians on this point, see Lightfoot's note on "The Later Visit of St. Paul at Jerusalem," in his Commentary, p. 91.

from the historical point of view. Paul's is specific, with one object in mind, his relation to the "pillars."

(c) Acts reveals no disharmony in the deliberations. Gal. ii. 14 *seq.* narrates a sharp rebuke by Paul to Peter (at Antioch afterwards), showing, however, an imperfect conversion on Peter's part to the more liberal view of the rights of Gentile converts. Here again Paul narrates a specific incident, with which Luke may not have been acquainted, or have had no occasion to mention.

(d) Galatians omits all mention of the Apostles' decision. This does not seem strange when it is remembered that this decision was of local and temporary significance. Paul does, however, make the general statement, "They added nothing to me."

The following agreements in the accounts should also be noticed:—(a) The places in question are the same,—Antioch and Jerusalem. (b) The chief persons concerned are the same,—Paul and Barnabas on the one hand, Peter, James, (and in Galatians) John, on the other. (c) The subject is the same,—the relation of the Gentile converts to the Jewish (Mosaic) law. (d) The result is the same,—the approval of Paul's work by the Jerusalem Apostles, the agreement that the Gentiles need not be circumcised, and that Paul and his converts have special regard to some points which will be likely to promote harmony.

If the conversion of Saul occurred in the year 35, then the first visit to Jerusalem would fall in 38, and the third visit to attend the apostolic council in 52. **With Barnabas,** the regular companion of Paul in his missionary labors, from the time when Paul and Barnabas were commissioned (Acts xiii. 2), until the "sharp contention" which occurred between him and Paul in regard to Mark (Acts xv. 36, *seq.*). Here Paul assumes a certain precedence over Barnabas. Earlier (Acts xi. xii.) Barnabas seems to have been the leader. **Titus also,** *i. e.* in addition to Barnabas. Titus is nowhere mentioned by name in the Acts, but is naturally included in the "certain others," (Acts xv. 2). This is the first appearance of Titus in the New Testament history, but numerous references to him are afterward found in II Cor., Titus, and II Timothy. He and Timothy were among the most trusted of the Apostle's helpers.

2. And I went up by revelation; and I laid before them the gospel which I preach among the Gentiles, but privately before them who were of repute, lest by any means I should be running, or had run, in vain:—By revelation: Such was the motive of the journey to Paul. To the church at large, he was chosen as a deputy, as Luke narrates; but, in his own thought, his going was in obedience to a "revelation," by which some inner experience of his own soul must be meant. What the form or mode of the revelation was, we do not know. *Cf*. in Acts. xxii. 17 his reference to the experience of a "trance" or ecstacy; also to that of a "vision" in Acts xvi. 9. In Acts xx. 23 he refers to an impulse of the Spirit, or a prophetic inspiration, in which the Spirit had taught him through the events that were happening, how critical would be his situation, on another occasion, in Jerusalem. **I laid before them the gospel which I preach,** which I continue to proclaim (κηρύσσω). This gospel was the doctrine of salvation through Christ alone, apart from obedience to the Mosaic Law. More specifically, it was justification by faith in Christ, as opposed to justification by works of meritorious obedience,—the Jewish idea. This gospel in the form in which he taught it among the Gentiles, in contrast to the Judaic phase of Christian teaching, with emphasis, no doubt, upon its universality and completeness in itself, he laid before **them who were of repute** (οἱ δοκοῦντες), *i. e.*, Peter, James and John. Why did he do this? The answer given is: **lest by any means I should be running, or had run, in vain.** Does this mean (*a*) in order to correct it by the authority of the "pillars"? *i. e.* lest it be found that, after all, he had made a mistake in his teaching. (So Tertullian, DeWette). This explanation would be contrary to the whole course of the argument,

The Approval of Paul's Gospel, etc.: ii. 2.

which assumes a revelation and fixed certainty as the warrant of his teaching. (*b*) He wished to come to an understanding with them, because the Jewish views which claimed to rest on their authority might thwart his labors and make his running in vain. Paul does this lest his labors be rendered unsuccessful (Lightfoot). (*c*) He laid his gospel before them in order to learn whether, perhaps, he was running in vain, not as indicating uncertainty on his part, but as desiring to satisfy their minds (Thayer's Lex. on μήπως, Meyer). View (*b*) takes the terms **lest by any means** (μήπως) as indicating purpose (= *ne forte*); view (*c*) as interrogative (= *num forte*). The word μήπως can be either telic or interrogative, and τρέχω (R. V. **I should be running**) can be either indicative or subjunctive.*
If μήπως is telic, then τρέχω is subjunctive; if interrogative, then it is indicative. To me the view (*c*) seems more probably correct. Paul's object was to secure their approval, not because he felt uncertain in regard to the success of his work, or feared opposition from them, but in order that it might be seen that in their view also he was not laboring in vain.

3. But not even Titus who was with me, being a Greek, was compelled to be circumcised.—The force of the argument is: But so

---

* In I Thess. iii. 5, we have a mixture of indicative and subjunctive constructions after μήπως.

far from it appearing that I was running in vain; so far from the Apostles at Jerusalem rejecting my gospel and disapproving my procedure; they did not even require the circumcision of Titus, my companion, which the Judeo-Christians, no doubt, desired and probably demanded. The Apostles did **not even** (οὐδέ) require this, which from a Jewish point of view would have been quite natural. According to this interpretation, the phrase **being a Greek** is concessive. Although he was a Gentile traveling with me in Judea, they did not require his circumcision. The implication seems to be that the circumcision of Titus had been demanded by certain Judaizers; the Apostles, however, did not enforce the demand. It would be clearly inconsistent with Acts xv. to suppose (with the Tübingen critics) that it was the Apostles who made this demand. Inasmuch as Titus was a Greek, they conceded, as against the extremists, that circumcision was unnecessary, and this concession was proof that in the judgment of the three, Paul was not running in vain, but was working in harmony with the divine plan in his Gentile ministry and in discountenancing circumcision for the Gentile convert. For Paul's conciliatory action in the case of Timothy whose mother was a Jewess, see Acts xvi. 1–3.

4. And that because of the false brethren privily brought in, who came in privily to spy out our liberty which we have

in Christ Jesus, that they might bring us into bondage.—The grammatical connection is loose throughout this and the following verses. The various interpretations of this verse may be summed up thus: (a) verse 4 gives the reason for the fact that Titus was not compelled to be circumcised, stating it rather on the side of Paul's non-permission of it (so Meyer). He was not compelled, that is, we did not permit him to be circumcised on account of the false brethren (the implied thought being that they had demanded it). (b) We should supply: **I permitted it.** Though the Apostles did not compel it, I allowed Titus to be circumcised on account of, as a concession to, the Judaizers (so Tertullian, Rückert). The fatal objection to this view is that it is wholly contrary to Paul's convictions upon the subject in question. Moreover, the very character of the persons making the demand would make the Apostle more inflexible in standing by his principles. (c) We are to supply: "The primitive Apostles advised me to yield, though they did not compel it; they advised me to make the concession to the weaker brethren" (so Lightfoot). The objection to this view is that it is contrary to the temper shown in the decree of Acts xv. 24–29, as well as grammatically quite arbitrary. The **false brethren** (*cf.* Acts xv. 1) were professedly Christians, who, however, maintained the erroneous idea that circumcision was necessary to salvation. Such were false to the distinctive principles of Christianity, salvation by grace through faith in Christ. There was a party of this kind in Judea who had thrown the church at Antioch, the chief sphere of their influence among the Gentiles, into great disturbance. They had taken pains to be present and to urge their Jewish opinions. They are designated as **brought in** (παρεισάκτους), illegitimately added, to the Christian brotherhood, to which they did not properly belong. The same idea is repeated in **came in privily** (παρεισῆλθον), making a play on words. They assumed toward the Pauline Christians the attitude of spies. The liberty in which Paul taught his converts to rejoice was freedom from the Mosaic law, deliverance from the moral bondage which it engendered, but was powerless to lift. This liberty they regarded with suspicion and restless hostility. They perpetually sought to construe it as laxness and unfaithfulness to the Scriptures. *Cf.* the testimony against Stephen of the witnesses who said that he had spoken against Moses and the Temple, Acts vi. 13, 14. "This they do," says the Apostle, "that they may bring us into bondage to the Mosaic law," that is, into the helpless and hopeless condition of those who make the futile effort to be saved by works.

5. To whom we gave place in the way of subjection, no, not for an hour; that the truth of the gospel might continue

with you.—This verse reaffirms, concerning the false brethren, what was already stated in verse 4, but in a changed construction, and with added emphasis upon the fact that he and his companions, Barnabas and Titus, did not yield to them in the least. The meaning is:—"Not even for an hour did we yield by (rendering) obedience (to their demand)." He refers here directly to the extremists, the **false brethren,** who demanded the circumcision of all Gentile converts: "We did not even (οὐδέ) yield for an hour." Note that the οὐδέ of ver. 3 repels the idea that the Apostles were hostile; that of ver. 5 emphasizes the determined attitude of Paul toward the Pharisaic party; as if he said: The "pillar" Apostles by no means opposed me, but as for the demands of the extremists, I gave them no consideration.

In the clause beginning, **that the truth,** etc. (ἵνα ἡ ἀλ. τοῦ εὐαγ.) he states the bearing of this action upon his Galatian readers. He affirms: "We maintained our ground thus firmly in order to conserve for you the distinctive truth of the gospel." The Galatian Christians, as being predominantly Gentile, would be directly included in their fixed purpose to maintain the principle of freedom from the law. We cannot well overestimate the importance of the Apostle's position upon the question at issue. He was the great champion of the independence, completeness, and sufficiency of Christianity. He declares that it does not need to be, and must not be, mixed up with Mosaism, of which it is the fulfilment, and from which it is free. It is difficult to see, humanly speaking, how the church could ever have freed itself from the leading-strings of Judaism, and how Christianity could have developed its own distinctive character, but for the work of some such man as Paul who clearly saw the issue and bravely faced it. It was a question between Christianity dominated by Jewish particularism, and Christianity for all men offered on moral and spiritual conditions. Well might the duty to secure the triumph of the latter conception have for Paul the character of a direct revelation.

6. But from those who were reputed to be somewhat (whatsoever they were, it maketh no matter to me: God accepteth not man's person)—they, I say, who were of repute imparted nothing to me.—The student of the original text will observe that the grammatical structure of verses 6–10 is very irregular. In verse 2 he had said that he laid his gospel before them who were of repute, but does not there proceed to state definitely what attitude they took in respect to it. Their verdict upon his teaching is taken up in verse 6, beginning with, **but from those,** etc., (ἀπὸ δὲ τῶν δοκ.), as if he would say: "but from those who were of repute, I received this reply or decision"; but at the expression, **those who were reputed to be somewhat** (τῶν δοκούντων εἶναί τι), he delays the completion of his statement to insert the parenthetical remark that it does not matter to him who they are, for God does not judge by rank or station, and when he resumes the statement as to what they said, he does so as if forgetting that he had started with the preposition **from** (ἀπό) and resumes the sentence in new form. (*Cf.* the paraphrase prefixed to Chap. II. Lightfoot has a clear paraphrase of verses 6-9, Commentary *in loco.*) **They, I say, who were of repute** (οἱ δοκοῦντες), better, perhaps, "those who are of repute" (in the judgment of the Galatians); "those who appear to you as something (great)." The expression is slightly ironical, not as reflecting upon the twelve themselves, but as reflecting upon those to whom the Jerusalem Apostles seemed to be such great authorities, in comparison with Paul himself. The parenthetical, **whatsoever they were** (ὁποῖοί ποτε ἦσαν), is thrown into the balance over against the Judeo-Christian attachment to the authority of the twelve. He says in effect: "Hold them in as high honor as you please; it does not matter how great their influence and authority; I am independent of them. God judges not by rank, but has chosen me as truly as he has them."

There are two interpretations of **whatsoever they** [then, ποτέ] **were,** etc. (1.) The adverb (ποτέ) has its usual temporal force, (= *olim*), "whatever they were *once*," the reference being to their personal knowledge of Christ on earth. [Beza renders, *olim*, the Vulgate, *aliquando*], (so Luther, Olshausen, Hilgenfeld, Wieseler, Ewald, Lightfoot).

It is favorable to this view that everywhere else in Paul the adverb (ποτέ) has its usual temporal force, though in classic Greek authors it is often equivalent to the Latin suffix *cunque*. (2.) The phrase means: "of whatever sort;" "whatever their pre-eminence or advantage" (= *qualescunque*). (So Meyer, Ellicott, Thayer's Lexicon, R. V.) If this is the correct interpretation of the phrase, it could mean, **whatsoever they were** in any one of several respects: (*a*) in having seen Christ, (comes to same meaning as view above), (so Augustine). (*b*) Whatever they were in respect to repute and influence, (Meyer). The past tense (ἦσαν) may be considered as favoring the first view (1.), but is not decisive, for "whatsoever they were" may be said of any time past, relative to the time of writing, the **were** (ἦσαν) pointing back from this time of writing to the time, for example, when he was in Jerusalem at the council, five or six years before. This (*b*) is, on the whole, the preferable view, as being most in harmony with the whole context and situation. He has no occasion here to refer to the remote past, but only to the alleged superiority of the twelve relatively to himself. The argument is:

"Whatever character you may, in your preference and prejudice, attach to them, it matters not to me; I have my authority unquestionably and directly from Christ." **God accepteth not,** etc. (πρόσωπον [ὁ] θ. ἀνθ. οὐ λαμβάνει): The expression, to accept the person or countenance, came into the New Testament usage through the Septuagint, for the Hebrew נָשָׂא פָנִים, to bear, receive, or accept the countenance, that is, to admit to favor (said, e. g. of kings in their relation to subjects), and so in the New Testament, "to show partiality to,"—a force which the Old Testament expression does not generally bear. Examples of the bad sense, which is found in the Old Testament, and which is the exclusive sense of the phrase in the New Testament, are found in Lev. xix. 15, Deut. x. 17. From this expression are formed the New Testament terms, "respecter of persons" (προσωπολήπτης, Acts x. 34) and "to have respect of persons" (προσωποληπτεῖν, Jas. ii. 9).

The New Testament bad sense is not, I think, to be attributed (with Lightfoot), to the fact that the word πρόσωπον at first meant a mask (and so came to stand for outward circumstances or appearances in general), but to the natural extension of the idea of showing favor to that of exercising partiality, a step of thought actually made in several Old Testament passages.

Imparted nothing to me, etc.—Now for the

first time is stated just what the primitive Apostles did or did not do in view of the explanation by Paul of his teaching (verse 2), and with the grammatical peculiarity that it is now introduced as a ground (γάρ) for the statement in the parenthesis that "God shows partiality to no one." The word rendered **I say** (γάρ) strictly assigns a reason for something that has been stated. The irregular construction of the passage gives rise to several interpretations of the word (γάρ). The proof that God does not show partiality is, that the other Apostles recognized his equality with themselves; they communicated nothing to him by way of supplementing his teaching (so Meyer). (*b*) The sentence assigns the reason for the statement, **it maketh no matter to me** (οὐδέν μοι διαφέρει); "it does not matter to me what preference you assign to the twelve, they, as a matter of fact, asserted no such pre-eminence by adding to my teaching," (so Alford). (*c*) The "for" may be considered as explicative; "to me it is certainly a fact, that whatever they have done for others, they have added nothing to my gospel," (so Ellicott). Meyer, in my judgment, takes the words naturally, and does not attempt to lessen the grammatical peculiarity. **They imparted nothing to me** (οὐδὲν προσανέθεντο) means, they did not supplement my teaching as if it needed correction or addition. This statement is the nerve of the whole argument, and constituted a complete refutation of the position of the Apostle's opponents and critics.

7. But contrariwise, when they saw that I had been intrusted with the gospel of the uncircumcision, even as Peter with the gospel of the circumcision.—So far from correcting my teaching, we came, continues the Apostle, to a good understanding and agreement. When they saw (probably as the result of Paul's explanations, or perhaps, from the known results of Paul's preaching) that his mission too was a divinely ordained one, and that they and he had been assigned by divine providence to different spheres of a common work. The expressions, **the gospel of the uncircumcision,** and **the gospel of the circumcision** (τὸ εὐαγ. τῆς ἀκροβυστίας,—τῆς περιτομῆς) are to be understood, not as different gospels, but as the one gospel defined according to these two spheres of its operation;—the Gentile and the Jewish world. The division of labor was not made on doctrinal grounds, nor was it strictly a geographical division, but rather an ethnographical one. The student of the original should notice that τὸ εὐαγγέλιον is accusative with the passive πεπίστευμαι, see Buttmann, p. 189. *Cf.* Rom. iii. 2, where λόγια is accusative, not nominative. Peter is singled out as the representative of the Jewish apostolate, for though he was the first preacher to the Gentiles (Acts xv. 7), his life-work, certainly up to this time, was chiefly among Jews, and in his sympathies he seemed to cling to the Jewish phase of Christianity.

8. (For he that wrought for Peter unto the apostleship of the circumcision wrought for me also unto the Gentiles):—He that wrought (ὁ ἐνεργήσας, *i. e.* God) **for Peter,** or in his behalf, *i. e.* to render successful the apostleship of the circumcision (*i. e.*, his work among the circumcised) wrought also for me, to the end of making successful my apostleship to the Gentiles. The exact carrying out of the parallelism would require "for the apostleship of the Gentiles." The dative **for Peter** is, as Ellicott explains, not governed by the preposition (ἐν) in composition with the verb (ἐνεργήσας,) since this verb is not a pure compound, but is dative *commodi*.

9. And when they perceived the grace that was given unto me, James and Cephas and John, they who were reputed to be pillars, gave to me and Barnabas the right hands of fellowship, that we should go unto the Gentiles, and they unto the circumcision.—The phrase **when they perceived** (γνόντες) takes up the thought and construction begun with **when they saw** (ἰδόντες) in verse 7. The **grace** which they perceived in Paul was the evident favor of God which had in their judgment authenticated his apostleship. It is noticeable that James here stands first, as Cephas certainly had at i. 18, 19. Some writers maintain that in matters relating to the apostolic College, Peter stands first, but in matters done at the Jerusalem church, James, its pastor, takes the pre-eminence. It is doubtful whether this distinction can be successfully defended for here certainly the act of the three is an act on behalf of all the Apostles present and of the whole council, and not of the Jerusalem church. In any case, James, the Lord's brother, rivalled Peter in prominence,—a distinction to which his relation to Jesus as well as his great zeal and excellence no doubt contributed. The point that he is not now called the Lord's brother, because between the first visit (i. 19) and this, James the son of Alphaeus had suffered martyrdom, making it unnecessary to distinguish this James, is better taken; but the omission is sufficiently explained by the simple fact that, having once given him this specific designation, it was not necessary to do so again in the immediate connection. In the word **pillars** (στῦλοι) is implied the figure of a building. These three Apostles had the reputation of being the chief supports of the church and they, no doubt, were the most prominent and influential of the apostolic company at that time; from our point of view, however, Paul surpasses them all in these respects. **Right hands of fellowship** (δεξιὰς κοινωνίας): The term **right hands** has no article because the phrase **to give right hands** (δεξ. διδόναι) is a stereotyped phrase. The phrase **of fellowship** is a defining genitive,—right hands expressive of fellowship. In the original text κοινωνίας is so far removed from δεξιάς in order to bring it near to the clause of purpose (ἵνα *seq.*) which follows, as indicating the meaning of the fellowship expressed. Thus the phrase **that we should go,** etc. (ἵνα *seq.*) logically depends upon the idea of **fellowship** and expresses the purpose of the agreement which was involved in the extension of the right hand, thus: "They gave us the right hand of fellowship expressive of the agreement that we go to the Gentiles, they to the Jews." In the final clause (ἵνα *seq.*), there is an ellipsis of the thought, **that we should go** (πορευθῶμεν), which the sense readily supplies. This general definition of the two spheres for the two branches of the apostolate in no way involved an exclusive adherence to Gentile communities for Paul. He never abandoned the maxim, "To the Jew first and also the Greek." (Rom. i. 16 *et al.*) The purpose of the council was met in reaching this general decision. Paul was to proceed with his work as before; so were the twelve. The council changed nothing. It approved Paul's ministry among the Gentiles, and proclaimed that the burdens which the extreme Jewish Christians wished to impose upon them should not be imposed. This decision was sufficient for Paul, both in respect to his public ministry, and in regard to his personal justification as a genuine Apostle.

10. Only they would that we should remember the poor; which very thing I was also zealous to do:—Only they would that (μόνον ἵνα, κ.τ.λ.): This clause depends upon the implied thought in the phrase "right hands of fellowship," in the same way as does the previous clause of purpose. They gave the right hand of fellowship expressive of agreement (in general) that, etc., only with this one specification **that we should remember the poor.** It is needless to supply any verb. This specific agreement to remember the poor related to the poor of Jerusalem and Judea. They were careful to insert among the terms this one limitation that Paul and Barnabas should not consider their Gentile apostleship as exempting them from securing aid for the poor of the circumcision; further than that they specified nothing. Their poverty was, no doubt, occasioned in part by persecution and perhaps also by the improvidence which the expectation of the speedy return of Christ had fostered (*cf*. II Thess. iii. 10-12), and probably, still further, by the working of the policy of a community of goods (Acts iv. 32-37). This remembrance of the poor is not mentioned in the Acts. It belonged to the more private compact made with the three. Paul had already (Acts xi. 29, 30) brought aid to the poor of Jerusalem, and they took a pledge of him that he would continue his interest and efforts, and he did so; *cf.* Acts xxiv. 17 (his fifth and last visit to Jerusalem). **Which very thing** (ὁ αὐτὸ τοῦτο); Note the emphatic repetition. The change from plural (**we should remember**) to singular (**I was zealous**), is probably occasioned by the fact that before any effort occurred to carry out the agreement he and Barnabas had separated (Acts xv. 39). Strictly speaking, we have no individual instance confirmatory of the words, **I was zealous** (ἐσπούδασα), because the case in Acts xi. 29, 30 occurred before the assembling of the council, and the others (I Cor. xvi. 3; Acts xxiv. 17) after the writing of the Epistle; (unless we suppose, with Lightfoot, that I Cor. was written before Galatians, in which case I Cor. xvi. 1-3 would be very much in point, since it would show that the Galatians themselves had shortly before the time of writing been solicited to contribute). We are probably to regard the cases mentioned as illustrations of the Apostle's practice and constant willingness in the matter.

II. Peter's Inconsistent Action at Antioch and Paul's Reproof of His Course, vv. 11-21.

11. But when Cephas came to Antioch, I resisted him to the face, because he stood condemned:—But when Cephas came to Antioch, etc.: After the council Paul and Barnabas returned to Antioch to deliver the decision (Acts xv. 30, *seq.*) and continued there for some time. During this sojourn, Peter came to Antioch,—a fact not mentioned by Luke. **I resisted him to the face** (κατὰ πρόσωπον αὐτῷ ἀντέστην), "I stood against him to the face," denoting the directness and sharpness of the reproof. Paul "faced" him in opposition and rebuke. The phrase κατὰ πρόσωπον does not mean "in the presence (of all)" (Erasmus, Beza), much less (= κατὰ σχῆμα), "in appearance" (Chrysostom, Theodoret). **Because he stood condemned** (ὅτι κατεγνωσμένος ἦν): The verb here used (καταγινώσκω) means to inquire into (judicially) *i. e.* to accuse or to condemn. Paul's strenuous opposition to Peter favors the stronger meaning here. "Because he was (or stood) condemned," not condemned by himself, nor by God, primarily, but by the Christian public of Antioch. The A. V. "was to be blamed," is too weak, and gives to the passive participle the force of the ending of the verbal adjective which it cannot bear. This translation resulted, perhaps, from a desire to minimize this difficulty between the Apostles.

12. For before that certain came from James, he did eat with the Gentiles: but when they came, he drew back and separated himself, fearing them that were of the circumcision:—For before that, etc., (πρὸ τοῦ γὰρ ἐλθεῖν); explanatory of Paul's opposition, and especially of the condemnation accorded to Peter. After Peter's vision (Acts x. 10, *seq.*), he had avowed the principle (x. 34, 35) that God is no respecter of persons, but that in every nation he that feareth him and worketh righteousness is acceptable to him, and had mingled freely in social intercourse with the converted heathen,—a proceeding which provoked objection from the Jewish party (Acts xi. 2, 3). Here at Antioch he was met again by the same criticism, and yielded to it. In so doing he acted contrary to the lesson of his vision. The objection rested on the Pharisaic distinction of clean and unclean which had been used against Jesus (Luke xv. 2), and which he had undermined by his teaching that not outward contact but inner character, thoughts, motives, and the deeds in which they issue, can defile a man. The lesson of the vision had been designed to abolish this distinction of clean and unclean (Acts x. 12–15). His action at Antioch was inconsistent with his former conduct which he had defended (Acts xi. 4, *seq.*). It was a yielding to Jewish prejudice and narrowness which Paul regarded as a violation of Christian principle, and a contradiction to Peter's position in the council where he had defended Gentile freedom and declared that God had put no difference between them and the Jews (Acts xv. 8–10). **He did eat with,** etc., (συνήσθιεν): The imperfect tense denotes his former customary action and included, if it did not chiefly refer to, the lovefeasts (ἀγάπαι), in connection with which the Lord's supper was observed. To make on these occasions the separation which Peter's conduct logically implied and recommended, was to divide the church in that symbol of fellowship which best signified its unity and brotherhood. The difference between Paul and the Jewish Christian party was not as to whether the Gentiles should receive the gospel, for all agreed in this; but it was, as to whether they must also embrace the Jewish religion by being circumcised and keeping the Mosaic law in addition to exercising faith in Christ. This was the practical question between Paul and the Judaizers.

The extreme Pharisaic party reasoned thus: "So long as they do not so obey the law, are they not unclean? How, then, can we associate with them? Must they not remain separate from us?" This view made full Christian fellowship dependent upon a ritualistic prerequisite. They acknowledged the Gentiles as Christians, but they had not been circumcised. They, therefore, denied them full fellowship. To this view James seems to have been, of all the apostolic company, the most inclined, although it is certain that he was ready to concede to Paul that the Gentile converts need not take upon them the burdens of the law. The point in regard to full fellowship had not been decided in the council, although the spirit of the decision certainly looked strongly toward equality and full fellowship of Jews and Gentiles. Paul must now carry this point on which Peter wavered, else all that had been gained might have been lost. The Judeo-Christian opinion was a weak one, springing from a defective appreciation of certain teachings of Christ and an imperfect understanding of the nature and destination of the gospel, but it was a natural one, and illustrates Christ's saying: "No one having drunk old wine desireth new: for he saith, The old is good" (Luke v. 39), indicating the slowness with which the Christian world was able to break loose from Jewish particularism, and to grasp the full import and scope of the truth that Christianity was not a patch to be sewed upon the old garment of Judaism, but a new and perfect garment, and that, since it was the fulfillment of the law and the prophets, it was complete in itself and must abrogate the Mosaic system.

The phrase **from James** (ἀπὸ Ἰακώβου) should probably go with **came** (ἐλθεῖν). These persons (*cf.* **them that were of the circumcision,** *infra*) had come down from Jerusalem to spy out the liberty of the Gentile Christians. It is not said that they were sent by James for this purpose (Meyer), but they may have been. If so, we may hold, (*a*) that they abused their mission, since it can hardly be supposed that James would feel called upon to institute such proceedings (*cf.* Acts xv. 24). Or, it may be thought that they were zealots for the law who represented the view of James in reference to the subject of *fellowship* with the uncircumcised. In either case they would not be strictly identical with the "false brethren" (ii. 4) who held that circumcision was necessary to salvation. **He drew back** (ὑπέστελλεν) **and separated** (ἀφώριζεν) **himself**: The imperfect tenses describe what he *proceeded to do*, as if he were gradually overcome by their persuasions and objections. **Fearing them,** *i. e.*, fearing to excite the displeasure and disapprobation of the Jewish Christians, who had come to Antioch from Jerusalem. The statement that Peter was overawed by the Pharisaic party, is Paul's version of Peter's action. To Peter it was doubtless only caution, or accommodation (which Paul also practiced), but to Paul it was cowardice and inconsistency, involving a breach of Christian principle, viz., the full access of the Gentiles to all the benefits of the gospel on the same conditions with the Jews, and consequently their equal rights to full Christian fellowship "apart from deeds of the law."

13. And the rest of the Jews dissembled likewise with him; insomuch that even Barnabas was carried away with their dissimulation.—He here states two circumstances which were, in great part occasioned by Peter's action:—(1) The Jewish Christians at Antioch who had formerly felt no scruple about mingling with the Gentile Christians, now followed Peter and those who had come from James, and thus a schism was produced. (2) Even Barnabas, Paul's companion, was carried away by their inconsistent action. Here again the conduct of these persons is referred to by Paul in his apology, which is not free from polemic, as **dissimulation,** hypocrisy (ὑπόκρισις). It did not have this character to Peter and the others. It was the result of human prejudice and weakness, and in the case of Peter, it was, as Calovius says, an *actio, non habitus*. It was, however, hypocrisy, in the sense that it was playing a part inconsistent with principles which they had formerly accepted and practiced; logically it was infidelity to Christianity which deserved unsparing rebuke. Peter's hypocrisy consisted in constraining the Gentile converts to act the Jew (Ἰουδαΐζειν) (v. 14), contrary to his previously avowed convictions. It is to be noticed that Acts and Galatians clearly represent his conviction as in agreement with Paul, and his Judaizing action as an inconsistency with that conviction, and not (as the Tübingen criticism assumes) that his Judaizing was according to his conviction, and his Pauline action an exception to his custom. Then all his ordinary action, as Acts and Galatians represent it, would have been "hypocrisy," and this withdrawal from the Gentiles his one act of perfect consistency. The Tübingen criticism here simply sets aside the testimony which the New Testament contains on the subject including that of Paul's most polemic letter, and replaces it by a subjective theory of its own. The "hypocrisy" ascribed to Peter does not necessarily imply a *conscious* inconsistency with principle, but it clearly designates Peter's action as really such, in the judgment of the Apostle to the Gentiles.

14. But when I saw that they walked not uprightly according to the truth of the gospel, I said unto Cephas before them all, If thou, being a Jew, livest as do the Gentiles, and not as do the Jews, how compellest thou the Gentiles to live as do the Jews?—They walked not uprightly (οὐκ ὀρθοποδοῦσιν, "to walk straight"): The figure is of keeping to a path or line, hence "to act rightly according to the gospel." This departure from gospel truth Paul rebukes *openly*, **before them all** (ἔμπροσθεν πάντων). Peter's attitude was public and far-reaching in its influence. Paul would rebuke it and show its inconsistency before the assembled Christian community at Antioch. **If thou,** the **if** supposes the case so well known to be true. The sense is: "You, Peter, are a born Jew; yet you are accustomed to live (ζῇς) in a Gentile manner (ἐθνικῶς) not as a Jew (Ἰουδαικῶς) that is, to do as Gentiles do in reference to such questions as this of eating with the uncircumcised. If, then, although you are a native Jew, you are wont to discard Jewish scruples, how can you justify yourself in now, by your example, constraining those who are not native Jews to adopt Jewish customs?" There are two degrees of inconsistency here: (1) that implied in the condition, his own inconsistency with himself; (2) that contained in the conclusion of the sentence, his effort to constrain the Gentiles into harmony with his scruples. Paul says in effect:—Your own customary action would not even warrant your constraining *Jewish* Christians to hold by Jewish scruples; much more is that action inconsistent which constrains *Gentiles* to do so. **Compellest** (ἀναγκάζεις), referring to that moral constraint which comes from example and influence. The action of Peter, by reason of his position, amounted to a constraining force in regard to such a vexed question as this, concerning which there was so much unclear discernment and blindly zealous prejudice. **To live as do the Jews** (Ἰουδαίζειν = "to play the Jew"). This word touches the heart of the question in dispute, a question almost of destiny for the early church. Must the Gentile converts also become Jews? Must Christianity have Judaism added to itself before it became the perfect religion? Was Christianity thus deficient? Paul resisted this view and the course of Christian history justified his position.

Vvs. 15-21 are general statements, but are addressed to Peter, not to the Galatians, to whom he directly turns only at iii. 1. The object of Paul in these verses is to show that although Jewish Christian converts like himself and Peter belong to the so-called chosen people, yet, as a matter of fact, in becoming Christians they have confessed that salvation is not by their law, but only by Christ, and this step logically involves the uselessness for the attainment of salvation of all legal works and the wrong of imposing them on Christians. Paul opposes to Peter's action, not merely arguments, but the whole nature and meaning of the Christian life upon which Peter has himself entered.

15. We, being Jews by nature, and not sinners of the Gentiles, may be regarded as a concessive conditional sentence to which v. 16, *seq.*, forms a conclusion, thus:—(ver. 15) "True, we are born Jews, and not Gentile 'sinners,' as we native Jews are accustomed to call them; (ver. 16) yet we have broken with our old religion, and have taken the ground that salvation is through Christ alone. How inconsistent then to impose the burdens of that system which we have ourselves resigned upon ourselves and our converts. If you, Peter, put a high price upon Jewish privileges and connections, I have to remind you that we have voluntarily surrendered them in becoming Christians, and that we cannot go back to them without falseness to our Christian decision and position." There is a touch of subtle irony in verse 15. If the Greek language had possessed quotation marks, the word "sinners" (ἁμαρτωλοί) would, no doubt, have been designated by them, since the word voices the popular Jewish idea of the Gentiles.

16. Yet knowing that a man is not justified by the works of the law, save through faith in Jesus Christ, even we believed on Christ Jesus, that we might be justified by faith in Christ, and not by the works of the law: because by the works of the law shall no flesh be justified.—The first part of this verse illustrates a mixture of two constructions. (1) "A man is not justified *except through* faith," and (2) "A man is not justified *by works of law but by* faith." We have a combination of these two: "A man is not justified *by works of law except through* faith." * **The works of the law** (ἔργα νόμου), *i. e.*, deeds of obedience to the Mosaic law contemplated as a ground of acceptance with God. The real reason for this denial of their justifying power is found in Rom. viii. 3. There are two conceivable modes of salvation, (*a*) that by

---

* The two constructions in Greek would be: οὐ δικαιοῦται ἀνθ. ἐὰν μὴ διὰ πίστεως, and, οὐ δικ. 'ανθ. 'εξ ἔργων νόμου ἀλλὰ διὰ πίστεως. In the mixed construction of the text ἐὰν μή logically belongs not to the whole preceding sentence, but only to οὐ δικαιοῦται.

works or merit, on the principle of *quid pro quo*, in which case a man "hath whereof to glory" (Rom. iv. 2); and (*b*) that by grace through faith, trust or self-surrender. We Christians, says Paul, have abandoned the former principle as impracticable on account of the power of sin which dwells in the flesh, and which prevents our perfect fulfillment of the law's requirements, without which justification by its deeds is impossible, and have adopted the other. **Even we** (καὶ ἡμεῖς), Paul and Peter, who are genuine Jews. This lays emphasis upon the *personal* acceptance by Peter and Paul of the principle of justification by faith only. In believing on Christ we have broken with the old system and have renounced the possibility of salvation in the way in which we formerly held it as Jews. We are committed to the way of faith as the way to justification. Notice the two forms of thought, **through faith** (διὰ π.) and **by faith** *i. e.* "from" or "out of" (ἐκ π.), the former denoting the relation of faith as that through the operation of which the righteous state is entered, the latter designating the righteousness as originating in faith. This last phrase cannot mean, however, that faith is the producing source of righteousness, which is always a "righteousness which comes from God as its source" (δικαιοσύνη θεοῦ, Rom. iii. 21), but signifies the procuring cause on man's part, so that righteousness is said to proceed from faith in the sense that it is attained in the line of faith (as opposed to works). Paul ordinarily uses the former phrase; the latter (ἐκ πίστεως) perhaps arising as correlative to "from works," 'εξ ἐργων (as here), or more probably as conforming to the Septuagint translation of Paul's favorite text (see Rom. i. 17). The phrase "upon faith" (ἐπὶ τῇ πίστει) also occurs (Philip. iii. 9). **By the works of the law shall no flesh be justified,** assigns the Old Testament authority for our knowledge that a man is not justified by legal observance and for our consequent action in adopting another principle. So Wieseler, Lightfoot, Ellicott, vs. Meyer, who argues from the absence of a formula of quotation, and from the variation of the words from the supposed quotation (Ps. cxliii. 2) that no Scripture proof is intended. But the variation of the words from the LXX. (οὐ δικαιωθήσεται ἐνώπιόν σου πᾶς ζῶν, *cf.* our text) is much less marked than is frequently the case in Paul's quotations, and it is by no means a universal habit of Paul to use a formula of quotation. *Cf.* Rom. iii. 20 where the same words with the addition of "before him" (ἐνώπιον αὐτοῦ) are used in proof, and without any formula of quotation, and concerning which Meyer says (*in loco*) that Paul has Ps. cxliii. 2 in mind. If so there, why not here also? On the use of this passage I would remark: (1) Literally translated, it would be, "For before thee, no man living is righteous" (Toy, Perowne). The LXX. renders

(כִּי לֹא־יִצְדַּק לְפָנֶיךָ כָל־חָי) "shall not be justified," etc. (οὐ δικαιωθήσεται) and this meaning is followed by both our English versions. (2) The Psalm passage refers to the universal sinfulness of men. "Enter not into judgment with thy servant, for no living man stands blameless before thee." Paul by connecting the expression with the phrase, "by works of law," (both here and in Rom. iii. 20), has applied the passage to justification by faith. (3) The term "all flesh" (πᾶσα σάρξ = כָּל־בָּשָׂר) is a familiar Hebraism for the actual Septuagint reading (πᾶς ζῶν). The construction "all flesh shall not be justified" (οὐ δικ. πᾶσα σάρξ) is an exact imitation of the Hebrew construction, and means "no flesh shall be justified" or "no one shall be" (οὐδεὶς δικαιωθήσεται). The negative οὐ is to be understood as standing in closest connection with its verb.

Respecting the Pauline doctrine of justification, it should here be observed (1) that the word "justify" (δικαιοῦν) in the New Testament is connected through the LXX. with the causative forms (Hiphil or Piel) of the Hebrew verb meaning "to be righteous" (צָדַק) which prevailingly mean in the Old Testament, "to declare, or pronounce righteous," "to acquit from guilt and blame." "To justify" is, with Paul, a forensic term, and accordingly justification is expounded by judicial analogies chiefly. (2) "Righteousness" (δικαιοσύνη) is the *status* or character of one whom God thus pronounces just (δίκαιος). He is acquitted, forgiven, declared free. His relation to God is now denoted by "righteousness." (3) Faith in Christ is the condition on which God pronounces the judgment of justification. Paul's usual statement is that faith is reckoned to the believer "for righteousness" (εἰς δικ.). (See especially Rom. iv). The two expressions, "faith is reckoned," and "righteousness is reckoned," are synonymous. The meaning is that, on condition of faith, God regards and treats the sinner as if righteous, as if he was what he ought to be; or, in other words, righteousness is reckoned to him, set over to his account. This means that faith is that attitude of mind and heart which makes it possible for God to treat the sinner so much better than he deserves as to acquit him before the law and pronounce him righteous, though, from the standing-point of his mere personal merit, he is not yet such. (4) The righteousness of Christ is never said to be imputed to the believer, not even in Phil. iii. 9, where the Apostle explains the "righteousness of his own" by calling it "a righteousness which is by the law." The doctrine of the imputation of Christ's righteousness has been obtained by carrying out and developing the analogies which constitute the form of Paul's thought into a full system. This theological formula rests upon inferences drawn from Paul's language, and is to be distinguished from the Pauline doctrine proper, in which no statement which is the equivalent of it is found. (5) The interpretation which gives full weight to the legal or juridical form of Paul's teaching concerning justification, is the correct one. It is possible, however, to lay an undue stress upon the formal element of Paul's doctrine, the Jewish moulds into which it was run, and not enough upon its substance, the ethical and spiritual truths which are the content of its outer form. May not theology distinguish between the inherited Jewish moulds of Paul's thought, and the vital and essential truths which those moulds contain? It seems to be the excessive emphasis of legal analogies in this sphere of doctrine which has imparted to the Protestant doctrine of justification, in the judgment of many profound theologians, an appearance of arbitrariness and even of injustice, according to which righteousness is merely the result of a declaration and not an ethical reality. To such a one-sided view, we think, a candid study of Paul's teaching, as a whole, will not lead.

(6) Many modern theologians, in their reaction from the formal, judicial aspect of justification, have erred as much in regard to exegetical exactness as the older Reformed theologians sometimes did in doctrinal formalism and one-sidedness. While the latter identified Paul's Jewish thought-forms with the whole truth, and then built wholly upon them, the former have commonly over-

looked them, or have subjected the Apostle's language to unnatural interpretations in order to eliminate this element. It is desirable to expound the moral and spiritual truths and experiences which form the content or ethical counterpart of Paul's legal system, but exegesis is, first of all, a study of form, and must not, for any supposed or real theological interest, eliminate or disregard the peculiarities of the writer's modes of thought and expression, however subordinate it may suppose them to be to the spiritual facts involved. The error, on the one side, is in supposing it necessary to limit all theological thought to the Jewish thought-forms of the Apostle Paul; that, on the other, lies in not acknowledging and emphasizing those thought-forms just as they are. I venture to think that what is needed, both for theology and exegesis, is a clearer perception of the Jewish formal element in Paul's modes of thought and argument and an equally clear discernment and recognition of his clear, strong grasp upon the facts of the spiritual life which correspond to the judicial processes through which, in accord with his Jewish training, he conceives of the believer as passing. The figurative language, the analogies which the Apostle draws from the law or the current thought of his time, are of first importance for exegesis, while for theology they yield to the deeper truths of spiritual life and experience which they serve to illustrate or convey.

17. But if, while we sought to be justified in Christ, we ourselves also were found sinners, is Christ a minister of sin? God forbid.—Paul is still engaged in refuting Peter's position. There are two interpretations of the word **sinners** (ἁμαρτωλοί): (a) It is the same as in ver. 15, sinners from the Jewish point of view (= Gentiles). (b) It means primarily sinners in fact, as opposed to "righteous" (δίκαιοι). If the former interpretation be given, the protasis of the sentence would seem to mean, "If when seeking to be justified in Christ, even we ourselves (Jews) were found to be 'sinners' (i. e. to stand on the same level as the Gentiles), then might not one conclude that Christ is the minister of sin? We abandon the law and betake ourselves to Christ. We confess the inadequacy of our legal righteousness, and resort to Christ for justification, but in vain. We find ourselves on the plane of Gentile 'sinners' and that is all." Perhaps it might be said that Christ was responsible for that failure, and is thus a minister of sin (an illogical conclusion), (so Lightfoot). This view lays the main emphasis in the word "sinners" on the idea of *sinners from the Jewish point of view,* meaning those who have abandoned the law.

If on the other hand the word **sinners** means primarily sinners really, *i. e.* before God, unjustified men, as opposed to "righteous," the sense would seem to be: If our effort to be justified in Christ left us just where we were before, would not Christ be a minister of sin because he led us to abandon our efforts to obtain legal righteousness, and then did not safely conduct us to the goal by any other way? The Apostle then answers:—Let this conclusion never be drawn; *i. e.* the supposition on which it rests is false. Christ does not leave us sinners as he found us, but leaves us "just" (δίκαιοι). (So Meyer, Ellicott). In this case the words **God forbid** (μὴ γένοιτο) negative the whole verse; in the other view, they negative only the illogical conclusion sought to be based upon the supposition made. In the former case the question: Is Christ a minister of sin, supposes a distinctly negative answer. In the latter, it indicates what is a plausible but erroneous conclusion from premises in themselves correct. What is the bearing of these explanations upon Paul's refutation of Peter? On the former interpretation he seems to be charging upon Peter the assertion or admission of this false conclusion that Christ is a minister of sin, and assumes that Peter's abandonment of his ordinary conduct, ("living as do the Gentiles," ver. 14), is equivalent to the confession that he acted wrongly in forsaking the law and attaching himself to Christ. He thus brought himself down upon the plane of Gentile "sinners." This view seems to me far-fetched. The emphasis of Paul's thought does not rest upon the question whether it was sinful to abandon the law or not, but upon the question whether faith in Christ was attended with success or failure. Peter had acted as if it were a failure, and thereby gave color to the idea that Christ left those in sin who applied to him for salvation. The whole force of the verse is aimed at Peter's action which involved the idea that justification by faith in Christ was not perfectly successful and complete. Lightfoot's exposition of the views which he rejects seems to me unsatisfactory, because he treats them as if all turned on the one point of the sinfulness of abandoning the law ; whereas the thought is, whether Christ leaves men unjustified sinners, requiring still to observe the law to complete their salvation. It is this idea which Paul negatives, as well as the conclusion (**Christ a minister of sin**), which might be drawn from it. This view alone places the right emphasis and sets the verse in its true relation to Peter's inconsistency. Paul's thought is that Peter has acted in such a way as to make plausible the idea that Christ could not justify; that he was a helper to sin rather than to righteousness. *Cf.* Meyer *in loco*.

The following particulars should be further observed; **While we sought** (ζητοῦντες) is emphatic by position, and is in itself an emphatic expression for the idea of believing, in order to make the antithesis to the result supposed (**were found sin-**

ners) the sharper: "If after our effort to be saved by faith, it turns out that we are after all only sinners still." **In Christ,** (ἐν Χριστῷ) while substantially equivalent to "through Christ" (διὰ Χριστοῦ) is different in form, and should be noted as a mark of Paul's conception of the believer's vital personal relation to Christ in justification which is less in the foreground in his formal discussion of the doctrine of justification, but which predominates in his language touching the Christian life. It shows the reality of the spiritual groundwork and counterpart of Paul's juristic theology. Justification is, in the terms of Paul's system, a sentence pronounced on condition of faith which ushers the believer into a new state and relation to God; but it is also that new character in Christ which springs from the appropriation of the person and spirit of Christ in love and trust. The sentence or verdict has new spiritual relationship, vital fellowship with Christ and newness of personal life, as its essential spiritual content. It means not merely new standing, but new heart. This latter is the reality, the life and substance which fills the Jewish inherited mould of the Apostle's thought. As exegesis must not slight the latter, so must theology and practical religious thought dwell much upon the former. **Were found sinners** (εὑρέθημεν ἁμαρ.) forms the counterpart to **while we sought.** "If after all our seeking we were found to be," etc. The verb refers to the ascertaining of a result in experience (*cf.* Rom. vii. 10); "if it has turned out that," etc. The word expresses the idea that the supposed case would be something *surprising*, which already creates a presumption against the supposition made. **We ourselves** (καὶ αὐτοί), would, on Lightfoot's interpretation, emphasize Peter and Paul *as Jews*. On the other interpretation the idea would be: If even we Apostles and *Christian leaders* are still left unforgiven sinners. The student of the original text should note the force of ἄρα (unrepresented in our translations). It is an interrogative particle, expressive of anxiety or hesitation and is here slightly ironical. "Would it then follow? Some might easily suppose so."

Minister of Sin:—Sin is here used in almost a personified sense. It is the contrast to righteousness in its objective, forensic meaning. If Christ does not work in the sphere of righteousness, then he works in its opposite sphere, promotes sin, by leaving his adherents under its power, and thus helps it on. To such a supposition or question, Paul replies by his characteristic, "Let it not be" (μὴ γένοιτο) found here, as always, after an interrogation.

18. For if I build up again those things which I destroyed, I prove myself a transgressor.—The meaning may be thus represented: Why do I say that justification in Christ is no failure, and that Christ is no minister of sin? I say so because the real transgressor of the law is he who goes back from its fulfillment to its letter, who turns away from what the law pointed to, *i. e.* Christ, who is its end. He is the man who really breaks the law, because he fails to appreciate its deepest providential purpose. He is like one who gathers up the fragments and husks from which the fully ripe fruit had been taken out, and tries to combine them and keep them, instead of seeking and prizing the fruit. This passage thus intimates how the law is dishonored by those who place it above, or on a par with, the gospel. The charge of "transgression" falls not on Christ, but on the one who thus goes back to the law and deserts Christ who is its fulfillment. The case is made more vivid by the use of the first person (*cf*. Rom. vii.) **I build up again** (πάλιν οἰκοδομῶ) refers to the effort to set up the authority of the law as of perpetual obligation, as Peter was logically doing by his "dissimulation." **I destroyed** (κατέλυσα), refers to the renunciation of the law as a ground of justification. Paul is fond of the figure of a building. The verse describes the tendency of Peter's conduct and charges him with the grave mistake of trying to re-instate in authority a system which was fulfilled and done away in Christ, and therefore with falseness to his Christian position. The remaining verses elaborate the idea of the sole sufficiency of Christ for salvation.

19. For I through the law died unto the law, that I might live unto God.—Paul now adduces as proof of the statement in verse 18 his own actual experience. **I through the law** (ἐγὼ διὰ νόμου); **Law** here means the Mosaic law. "I died to the law," *i. e.* ethically; I became in relation to the law as a dead man; I broke all relation with it in becoming a Christian. *Cf.* Rom. vii. 4, where the dying to the law is illustrated by the dissolution of the marriage bond by the death of one of the parties. *Cf.* "the world hath been crucified to me and I unto the world," (vi. 14). But how did I die to the law (*dat. commodi*) by means of the law? The steps of thought implied in this condensed formula are found in Rom. vii. 7 *seq.*, (*a*) The law quickens sin, "By the law is the knowledge of sin." The law awakens the consciousness of sin and shows man his guilt. It shuts him up under sin that he may be delivered by Christ. (*b*) The law thus has a part in the work of salvation, but it is negative and preparatory. It slays men ethically, that is, in respect to their self-righteousness, in order that they may be ready to live by faith. (*c*) Thus the law leads men to Christ, which involves a breaking off of relations to itself. The law contributes to its own renunciation by leading to Christ for salvation. The connection of thought here is : The reason why I say that he most truly observes and honors the law who does not seek to be justified by it or regard it as essential, is that the law itself, in God's providence, serves the purpose of leading men to Christ for salvation instead of to itself. The purpose of this dying to sin, to the world, to the law, (all equivalent ideas though differing in form) is to live a higher life, **unto God.** *Cf.* Rom. vii. 4.

20. I have been crucified with Christ; yet I live; and yet no longer I, but Christ liveth in me: and that life which I now live in the flesh I live in faith, the faith which is in the Son of God, who loved me, and gave himself up for me.—Here we observe the bold figure of dying and living again carried out more specifically under the terms of crucifixion. The motive of this mode of representation is to be found in the fact of Christ's sacrificial death for us. That, as the ground of our new life, is easily spoken of, in a figurative manner, as that in which our ethical death to sin and life to God are included. The figure is based upon an identification of things which are causally and vitally related. The thought is: "I died when Christ died." "If one died for all, then all died," II Cor. v. 14; and Rom. vi. 8. (Note the Aorist here, expressing a definite past fact). These forms of thought illustrate Paul's mystical realism. All natural humanity sinned when Adam sinned (Rom. v. 12 *seq.*). All spiritual humanity died (to sin) when Christ died, was crucified with him, was raised (ethically) when he was raised. (Rom. vi. 5–6). This is an intensely realistic way of expressing the consequences of fellowship with Christ. When the perfect is used in these expressions (*e. g.* **I have been crucified,** *cf.* vi. 14) it denotes the abiding fact of fellowship. But the force of the Aorist should be noted in Rom. iii. 23; v. 12; vi. 8; and Col. iii. 3, signifying a definite action conceived as occurring at a definite past time; *e. g.* "All sinned when Adam sinned"; "All died when Christ died." These two forms of representation are the same, and should be understood in the same mystical manner. Paul carries out the figure of dying with Christ by representing the Christian in his transition to his new life as being buried with him, and as rising with him from the grave, and in some passages complicates this representation by joining with it the figures of baptism: Rom. vi. 4; Col. ii. 12.

Yet I live (ζῶ δέ) has this force: I spoke of dying to sin and living to God, but (δέ) this living is not the old natural life which indeed I once lived (Rom. vii. 9 "I was alive apart from the law once"), but a new life in Christ. By the emphatic **I** (ἐγώ), he means the self which previous to his conversion struggled vainly with sin (Rom. vii. 15 *seq.*) the "old (unregenerate) man" (Rom. vi. 6). The living is no longer that of my natural unrenewed self; that has died, and a new life in fellowship with Christ, nay, a living of Christ in me, has begun. "Christ liveth in me," that is, through the union of faith and love. The fellowship of life is such that Christ may be said to dwell and live in me. The reception of the mind and spirit of Christ is referred to (*cf.* Phil. i. 21: "For to me to live is Christ"). Both the expression: **I live** and **Christ liveth** have emphatic positions. The subsequent statement: **and that life which I now live** *seq.*, explains the meaning of Christ living in him. The word rendered "and" (δέ) is mildly adversative, thus: I do not mean to say by my strong language that I have wholly ceased from the natural life, but, so far as I am still in it, I have a higher stimulus and principle animating me, namely faith. It thus marks the limitation upon the strong statements going before.

In the Greek text the neuter pronoun (ὅ) is cognate accusative, as in Rom. vi. 10 (ὃ γὰρ ἀπέθανεν); not "in that he died" (A. V.) but "the death which he died" (R. V.). **Now** (νῦν) marks the contrast between the life which he is at present living in Christ, and the natural life which he formerly lived. **The flesh** (σάρξ) is here used in its primary meaning where it is equivalent to this weak, material form of existence, and not in the ethical signification so common with Paul where it denotes the natural unrenewed human nature. "Though I am still living the life of sense in this temporary sphere of perishable, material elements, my chief life element is not connected with this sphere, but with a higher. I am in a real sense 'in the flesh' but, in a deeper sense, am living 'in faith,' because it is in the faith-fellowship with Christ that my life-interests are found."

This faith he now traces to its basis. It is **in the Son of God** (genitive of the object) **who loved me,** etc. The object of his faith is the divine Son who from love gave himself up to suffering on his behalf (ὑπὲρ ἐμοῦ). This love is the motive of the giving and the warrant of faith. Faith is the human counterpart of the self-revealing, self-imparting love of God; the attitude of receptiveness, gratitude and trust toward that love which has evidenced itself in history most signally in the sacrifice of Christ. In Christ faith has the pledge of the divine love of which it may lay hold. The sacrificial work of Christ springs out of the self-imparting love of God and is the revelation of that love in its totality, both on the side of its vicariousness and sympathy, and on the side of its self-preservative quality, that is, its righteousness which is the self-respect of perfect love. The gift was of Himself. Self-giving is the deepest and truest giving. **For me,** *i. e.* on my behalf (ὑπέρ, as always with Paul when speaking of the vicarious work of Christ for men, except, possibly, I Thess. v. 10, where many texts and MSS. read περί; ἀντί is never so used). Paul, in the vividness and intensity of his interest in Christ's love and self-giving, speaks of it as done for him personally.

21. I do not make void the grace of God: for if righteousness is through the law, then Christ died for naught.—One final stroke at Peter's conduct. "I do not nullify the grace of God which has been revealed in Christ by going back to the legal system (as the conduct of the Judaizers practically does). **Grace** ($χάρις$) is the term which expresses the character of the Christian system as opposed to the legal system of commandment and of a corresponding obedience establishing merit. To go back to these is to desert and to set at naught the distinctive principles of grace and faith as applicable to salvation." **For if** ($εἰ\ γάρ$) explains and justifies this bold statement. "I speak of such Judaizing conduct as a setting at naught of God's grace as revealed in Christ, for it treats it as if it were not necessary. If men can be justified by the law, there is no need of the way of grace through Christ, and Christ died in vain.

But it is an axiom with all Christians that Christ did not die in vain. This was so even with the Judaizing Christians. If then he did not die in vain, he must have died because it was necessary, *i. e.* to open a way which the law did not and could not open. Thus Paul proves his point against Peter and the Judeo-Christians generally. Their conduct logically involves the putting of a light estimate upon Christianity, and regarding the death of Christ as needless. The argument is a *reductio ad absurdum* from the Christian point of view.

It has been concluded from this and similar passages that the genesis of Paul's doctrine of the insufficiency and temporary character of the law is here shown. It is an inference from the axiom that Christ's death must have been necessary (so Pfleiderer). But the Apostle is not tracing the logical genesis of his own thought here, but conducting an *argumentum ad hominem* against Peter from an assumption which Peter, equally with himself, would be compelled to grant. How Paul reached that axiom is in no way indicated. He is simply showing that Peter's Judaizing is inconsistent with the Christian view of Christ's death, not that his own view of the law sprang from that view of Christ's death.

The contrast of the law and the gospel is sharper in Galatians than in Romans because of the Judaizing tendencies and the suspicion concerning his apostleship in the Galatian churches. The two are pictured as mutually exclusive, not in their inherent nature, but with reference to becoming methods of salvation. In the divine intention of the two systems there could be no disharmony according to

Paul's premises, since the law-system was quite subordinate and preparatory to the gospel and could by no means come into rivalry with it. The mutual exclusiveness arises only in the false application and wrong adjustment of the two which those make who seek to hold both systems at once, and to combine the characteristic principles of both, works and faith, and make them equally essential conditions of salvation.

ANALYSIS AND PARAPHRASE OF CHAPTER III.

1. *The antagonism between the teaching of the Judaizers and the gospel of Christ,* vv. 1-14. You Galatians have been drawn away as if by magic from the truth so plainly taught you that you were saved through Christ's death (1). Reflect whether when you were converted, you received the gift of the Spirit by the doing of meritorious works, or by obeying the call to simply believe on Christ. Of course, the latter was the case. Will you, then, after having begun the life of the Spirit, fall back upon that lower plane where the flesh is the ruling element of life,—a power from which the law is unable to deliver you (2, 3)? What folly to endure persecution for the gospel, when you do not really remain true to it (4)! Have not all your spiritual gifts come to you in the line of faith, and not of works? Be true, then, to this principle and renounce the rival and futile principle of legal works of merit (5). From the typical case of Abraham you may learn the truth which I am urging. He was not justified by works, but by faith; now all

believers are his spiritual sons and are saved in the same manner (6, 7). The Old Testament recognizes the universal validity of the principle of faith (8, 9). On the contrary, those who stand upon the plane of law and seek to be saved by obedience to it will fail, for an absolutely perfect performance of all that the law requires is necessary in order to justification by law, and that man can never render (10). The law-principle says: Do all that the law requires and thou shalt live; the faith-principle says: Trust in God and thou shalt live. These indicate two different methods of salvation and the Scripture sanctions the latter as the only practicable one (11, 12). So far from having hope of being saved by the law, man had fallen under its curse and was helpless, but Christ, by taking the curse upon himself, freed us from it, that we might be justified and saved simply by trusting in him and his work for us (13, 14).

2. *The principle of the gospel antedates and underlies the law*, 15-22. Even a covenant between men, when once ratified, no third party may annul or supplement with new provisions; much less may God's gracious covenant of promise with Abraham be affected in its conditions and provisions by any subsequent dispensations (15). Now the promise to Abraham's seed is fulfilled only in Christ, and thus an identity and continuity of principle exists between that ancient covenant and the Christian

Analysis and Paraphrase of Chapter III. 105

gospel (16). Now the law which was given so long subsequent to this "proto-gospel," cannot affect its validity or change its provisions (17), and since salvation cannot be both by works and by faith, we must adhere to the more original and fundamental principle (18). What purpose, then, did the law serve if not that of justifying men? It showed them their need of justification and the impossibility of themselves attaining it, because it made them conscious of the depth and heinousness of their sins; thus this divinely ordained system was designed to lead men to Christ for salvation, rather than to be itself a means of saving them (19). It was a dispensation given to men through the agency of Moses; it was mediate and conditional, therefore. But in giving the promise and so in promulgating the gospel of faith, God stands forth alone and acts in independence and sovereignty. Hence the promise stands on a higher plane than the law (20). But it does not follow from this difference that the two dispensations, and their characteristic principles, are in all respects contrary. The legal system is subordinate to the gospel, but it serves the ends of the gospel; it must be subordinate, for otherwise the gospel would not have been needed as a saving agency (21). But it serves the ends of the gospel by teaching men their sinfulness, putting them in the prison-houses of remorse and despair until they shall long for the gracious deliverance which Christ freely offers to those who trust in him (22).

3. *The disciplinary and preparatory office of the law*, 23–29. It was the office of the law to imprison us by its condemnation until we should be set free by believing on Christ (23). The law may be called our tutor who, by his stern discipline and chastisement, prepared us for Christ and made us glad to find freedom and peace in him by faith (24). But now, as believers, we are no longer subject to this severe master, but possess the sense of liberty and sonship through Christ (25, 26). For truly all believers have entered into a unique relation to Christ which affects their whole attitude and standing. The distinctions of nationality, condition and sex are as nothing in the presence of that deeper unity which binds together all believers in Christ, so that all who believe, regardless of these distinctions, are really Abraham's seed (since Abraham's great significance was not in the fact that he was a *Jew*, but in the fact that he was a *man of faith*) and therefore inherit the blessings promised to him and to his seed in the covenant which God made with him (27–29).

CHAPTER III.

I. THE ANTAGONISM BETWEEN THE TEACHING OF THE JUDAIZERS AND THE GOSPEL OF CHRIST, vv. 1-14.

THE doctrinal statements of ii. 19-21 form a connecting link between the apologetic section and the distinctly doctrinal section (iii. 1-v. 12) of the Epistle. The Apostle does not develop his doctrine abstractly but in connection with the lapse of the Galatians into Judaism. Having proved the independence and divine authority of his apostolate, and shown that his doctrine alone is consistent with the sole sufficiency of Christ, he reproaches the Galatians with having fallen away from his teaching.

1. O foolish Galatians, who did bewitch you, before whose eyes Jesus Christ was openly set forth crucified?—He calls them **foolish** (ἀνόητοι), without mind or reason (νοῦς), irrational, undiscerning, easily duped by an unspiritual conception of life and salvation, readily yielding to the inconsistency and absurdity of the Jewish-

Christian position. He expresses his surprise and displeasure, both by the rhetorical question, **who did bewitch you?** and by the word **bewitch** (ἐβάσκανεν), which occurs only here and is apparently connected with φάσκειν "to talk," hence, "to use incantations," and so, in general, "to bewitch." It here denotes the subtle and radical character of the perversion and the dishonor connected with being thus misled. He regards this radical perversion as the more astonishing because he had set Christ clearly before them as the crucified one. He had preached the doctrine of the cross and its significance as involving the abrogation of the law and exclusive dependence upon Christ for salvation, so that he can say that he placed his cross before their very eyes, and yet they have surrendered and deserted him. The force of the preposition in composition (πρό) which is rendered **openly** (**set forth,** etc.) might either be temporal, "was formerly written (προεγράφη) in their hearts," *i. e.* the meaning of Christ's death was impressed upon them when he preached to them (so Meyer). The prevailing use of this verb (προγράφειν) in the New Testament favors this meaning (Rom. xv. 4; Eph. iii. 3). Or, it may be understood in a local sense, "was written before you," the figure being drawn from the posting of public notices, a frequent meaning of the word (so Lightfoot, Ellicott). The phrase **before whose eyes** (κατ' ὀφθαλμούς) lends some support to this more external figure, and the words **among you** (ἐν ὑμῖν, cf. A. V. and T. R.) which Meyer urges against it, are wanting in many important manuscripts (e. g. A B C ℵ cf. W. and H., Tisch. and R. V.) and, even if read, might mean " among you " (so our older version) as well as "within you" as in the expression: "The kingdom of God is within (or among) you" (ἐν ὑμῖν) Luke xvii. 21. The local force of the preposition in this particular case, gives a more vivid character to the passage, and more appropriately emphasizes the plainness with which Christ was set before them in the character of the crucified one, than would be done by the mention of the mere time relations, which would not be very essential here. This force of the words adds emphasis to the contrast between what they ought to have been and what they are. Both our English versions embody this interpretation. **Before whose eyes:** The phrase is emphatic, indicating the clearness of Paul's preaching on the point, which should have prevented such a result. **Crucified** (ἐσταυρωμένος) is an emphatic predicate defining more exactly and fully the phrase: **Jesus Christ was openly set forth.** It emphasizes that which was distinctive in Paul's preaching, and which stands in sharpest contrast to their present Judaizing. If the phrase "among you" is read, it is better to connect it with the verb **was set forth** than with the participle **crucified** (as commonly and in A. V.). He was set forth *among them* in the character of the crucified one.

2. This only would I learn from you, Received ye the Spirit by the works of the law, or by the hearing of faith?—Paul wishes now to point out their inconsistency, and this he will do by asking them one decisive question. **This only** (τοῦτο μόνον), *i. e.*, this question only as bearing upon the subject in hand, I would ask, and the answer will reveal your error. "Was it in the line of the law that you received the Spirit, or in the line of faith? On which of these contrasted principles did you begin the Christian life?" Of course the former was the case. Then why not remain faithful to the principle with which you started? **Learn** (μαθεῖν) is to acquire information, (= *cognoscere*); here it is half sarcastic, because Paul knew the necessary answer. I wish to confront you plainly, he says, with this alternative. **By** (lit. "from" ἐξ) **the works,** etc., **or by** (ἐξ) **the hearing,** etc.: The preposition denotes in each case, that by which the reception of the Spirit is mediated. Paul supposes two conceivable conditions on man's part of receiving the Spirit: (*a*) by doing works of law, so that these works of obedience may be contemplated as in a secondary sense the source (ἐξ) of the benefit derived; (*b*) by accepting the message of faith, in which case the

Spirit is received from, or as the result of faith. From which of these sources, in the line of which of these methods, did you receive the Holy Spirit? Here again it should be noted that receiving the Spirit is to Paul synonymous with justification. It will thus be observed that the juristic forms of thought are by no means exclusively employed. (*Cf.* again ii. 17, δικαιωθῆναι ἐν Χριστῷ). When discussing the contrast between faith and works Paul commonly employs the forensic language (see, especially, Rom. iv. *passim*), but here he does not. **The works of the law** (ἔργα νόμου), are works which the commandments of the law require, and which, in this connection, are conceived of as an alleged ground of meriting salvation. **The hearing** (ἀκοή) might be either (*a*), active "hearing" (Lightfoot, R. V.); or (*b*) passive, "report," "message" (Meyer, Ellicott, R. V. marg). It is indecisive to say (with Lightfoot) that (*a*) makes a better contrast with works of law, *i. e.*, the contrast between *doing* works and *hearing* faith, since the contrast is rather between the *principles* or *methods*, than between two specific actions like *doing* and *hearing*. Hearing is no more efficacious than doing. The contrast lies rather in the opposition between *law* and *faith*. New Testament usage favors (*b*) as does the natural force of "faith" (πίστις). On view (*a*) faith is conceived objectively as a thing heard,—not a characteristic Pauline conception. On view (*b*) the meaning is: "through the message which proclaimed faith as the essential condition of salvation." Faith is not with Paul primarily a doctrine, but an action, a thing to be done, a trust to be exercised. It was in the acceptance of the message which said: "Believe on Christ," that they received the Holy Spirit.

3. Are ye so foolish? having begun in the Spirit, are ye now perfected in the flesh?—The emphatic word, **so** (οὕτως) refers to the seriousness of the mistake of forsaking the gospel for the law. Then follows the statement of the inconsistency. The beginning spoken of (ἐναρξάμενοι πνεύματι) was the course of their Christian life up to the commencement of their Judaizing tendencies; the finishing (σαρκὶ ἐπιτελεῖσθε), is the course of their life since then as influenced by the false teachers. The contrast of **beginning in the Spirit** to being **perfected in the flesh** is parallel to that of "the hearing of faith" and "the works of the law" (verse 2). The terms rendered **Spirit** and **flesh** are in the dative case which here is instrumental and designates the character, principles, or qualities of the New and Old Testament systems respectively. **Flesh** (σάρξ) means the natural sinful character of men which the law cannot overcome. On the contrary the law but rouses this slumbering sin, and shows men how completely under the bondage of the flesh they are. (*Cf.* Rom. vii. 5, 6, where to be "in the flesh" (5), and under bondage to the law (6), are practically synonymous). "Will you, then," says the Apostle, "abandon the aid of the Spirit which you received by the message of faith, and try to work out your salvation on the plane of the law, giving yourselves up again to the government of the flesh?" If this view (substantially that of Meyer, Ellicott, Thayer's Lexicon and Julius Müller), be correct, then "the flesh" denotes the principle that obtains in the sphere of law, that dominates the natural man and defies the power of the law to break it. "Will you now try by means of the flesh to complete your Christian life, though all experience proves that the sinful flesh under the operation of law is the very power that crushes man and makes him powerless?" The difficulty with this interpretation is that "the flesh" is primarily connected with *man* as characterizing his unchristian life and action, and not with the *law* which we should here expect. Hence the majority of interpreters suppose that "the flesh" here stands as a designation of the law in its outward, ceremonial character (so Lightfoot, Rückert); most of whom find a reference either to circumcision or sacrifice. This view yields a meaning which, at first sight, seems more appropriate, but has decisive objections: (a) He would never characterize the law as such, by the word "flesh" ($\sigma\acute{a}\rho\xi$) it is rather "spiritual," "pneumatic" ($\pi\nu\epsilon\upsilon\mu\alpha\tau\iota\kappa\acute{o}\varsigma$), Rom. vii. 12–14. (b)

The habit of singling out the ceremonial and external features of the law in order to emphasize its inadequacy is a modern, not a Pauline one. (*c*) The Pauline usage of the word "flesh" (in contrast to "Spirit") is decidedly favorable to making it characterize man's state under the law, rather than the character of the law *per se*. If in Rom. iv. 1, the phrase "according to the flesh" (κατὰ σάρκα) is to be joined with the verb "hath found" (εὑρηκέναι), (as Meyer, Godet, rendering of the American committee in the R. V.), we then have in that passage a very similar thought and contrast between what Abraham found *apart from* and *in* faith.* The present tense in the phrase, **are ye now perfected,** enhances the irony; "Are you just now receiving the completion of your Christian life?"

4. Did ye suffer so many things in vain? if it be indeed in vain :—So many things in vain may be taken as an exclamation (so Meyer); or, as generally, may be understood interrogatively. **Did ye suffer?** (ἐπάθετε) is variously understood: in *good* (= to experience benefits), *neutral* (= to experience), or *bad* sense (= to painfully endure). The latter meaning is generally maintained and is required by the uniform use of the word in the New Testament and the Septuagint, as well as favored by the context (so Meyer, Lightfoot,

---

* Some critical texts, as that of Westcott and Hort, omit εὑρηκέναι altogether (*cf.* margin of R. V.).

Ellicott). What particular sufferings are meant? Interpreters reply: (*a*) Persecutions, such as overtook other Christians (II Cor. i. 8); though the New Testament says nothing of it among the Galatian churches (the commonest view). (*b*) It refers to the molestation of the Galatian churches by the Judaizers, and the imposing of unnecessary burdens upon them by these errorists (so Meyer). The sense requires that something be referred to which they had endured before, because of their devotion to Christianity. Was that suffering in vain? It was all for naught and might better not have been borne, if they were wrong in their exclusive adherence to Christ. The condition, **if it be indeed in vain** intimates Paul's opinion. They did right to suffer for their faith, because their faith was worth suffering for. But if they continue in this state of lapse, they would be confessing their former sufferings as vain and useless. Only the suffering of something which they endured at an earlier period because of their Christian faith, and rather than give it up, can satisfy the language. The meddling of the Judaizers was not of this character. The usual interpretation seems to me the preferable one.

5. He therefore that supplieth to you the Spirit, and worketh miracles among you, doeth he it by the works of the law, or by the hearing of faith?— He now resumes the contrast of law and faith which was drawn in verse 2, verses 3 and 4 being logically parenthetic. **He that supplieth to you the Spirit,** (that is, God). **Miracles,** (lit. powers δυνάμεις), might either mean miraculous *works* or miraculous *powers*. In the former case "among you" would be the proper rendering of the phrase ἐν ὑμῖν (so Winer); in the latter "in you" is the better translation (so Meyer, Ellicott, Wieseler). The verb **worketh** (ἐνεργῶν) in both its inherent meaning and regular New Testament use seems to favor the latter interpretation. In this case, the meaning would be: "He that bestoweth upon you the Spirit and worketh mighty powers within you." The reference is to the miraculous endowments so frequently spoken of in the New Testament, and which according to I Cor. xii. 28, were among the "gifts" which Christ entrusted to the church at his ascension. The sentence is elliptical and can be completed by supplying in indicative form the ideas of the participles **doeth he it?** etc. Of course, the answer to the question must be: He doeth it **by the hearing of faith.**

6. Even as Abraham believed God, and it was reckoned unto him for righteousness.—At this point, Paul brings forward the case of the believing Abraham to illustrate from the Old Testament itself the *principle* on which he was justified. It was not by works but by faith and you

The Judaizers and the Gospel, iii. 6. 117

are justified, he would say, in accordance with ($\kappa\alpha\theta\omega\varsigma$) the typical case of Abraham, by faith also. The passage is from the Septuagint of Gen. xv. 6, with the variation from the Hebrew of the passive ($\dot{\epsilon}\lambda o\gamma \acute{\iota} \sigma \theta \eta$) for the active: "He reckoned it to him" (וַיַּחְשְׁבֶהָ). The logical subject of **was reckoned** is "faith" ($\dot{\eta}\ \pi \acute{\iota} \sigma \tau \iota \varsigma$) or "believing" ($\tau\grave{o}\ \pi \iota \sigma \tau \epsilon \acute{\upsilon} \epsilon \iota \nu$). The preposition **for** ($\epsilon\grave{\iota}\varsigma$) is used with the predicative force so common in later Greek. The conception, well-nigh uniform with Paul, is that faith is that which is imputed, a formula which theology has sometimes repudiated lest to faith should be ascribed a *meritorious* character.* But this peril is better avoided by a right apprehension of the doctrine of faith than by a rejection of the Pauline formula. The very nature of faith excludes *desert* in the sense of a meritorious ground of salvation. Its very idea is receptiveness, trust and humble self-surrender, answering to the idea of "grace" ($\chi \acute{a} \rho \iota \varsigma$) on God's part, which is the idea of doing better for men than they deserve. Hence Paul's language does not and cannot mean that faith is reckoned for righteousness by reason of its inherent merit, as if it founded a claim upon God, but that, being an obedient and receptive attitude toward God and his salvation, it is the condition precedent

---

* *E. g.* in this statement: "He freely justifieth, * * * not by imputing faith itself," etc., Westminster Confession. xi. 1.

to our entering a right relation to God; so that, on the one hand, faith is distinguished from righteousness, contemplated as an *achievement by man*, a reward of merit; while, on the other hand, it may be reckoned as righteousness in the sense of *a gracious gift* because it is the act and spirit on man's part which receive the proffered righteousness in a consciousness of personal unworthiness. While therefore faith may be sharply distinguished from legal righteousness contemplated as a *quid pro quo*, it may be closely identified with righteousness considered as a gracious gift.

7. Know therefore that they which be of faith, the same are sons of Abraham.—The Apostle now develops his conclusion drawn from the *principle* contained in the Scripture cited. Since the significance of Abraham's religious life is found in faith, it follows that he is the typical father of the faithful; that sonship to him, in the spiritual sense, is determined by faith. The terms, **they which be of faith** (οἱ ἐκ πίστεως) is commonly understood as a contrast to lineal descendants, but its more exact counterpart would be (so Wieseler, Meyer), legalists, "those who are of works of the law," (οἱ ἐξ ἔργων νόμου, verse 10). The preposition "of" (ἐκ) has the same meaning as in verses 2–5; "those who proceed forth in their religious life from that principle."

8. And the scripture, foreseeing that

God would justify the Gentiles by faith, preached the gospel beforehand unto Abraham, saying, In thee shall all the nations be blessed.—This verse forms the transition to the proof that since believers only are sons of Abraham, they alone can share the blessing of justification promised to the nations in him. **Foreseeing** (προϊδοῦσα) implies a kind of personification of Scripture, based upon the idea of God as foreseeing what is promised in Scripture. The word rendered **would justify** (δικαιοῖ) is rendered by many "justifieth" (Meyer, Ellicott, R. V. marg.) and in that case denotes the *present* fact which Scripture foresaw as *future*. **Preached the gospel beforehand** (προευηγγελίσατο), declared the glad tidings in advance, viz., in the quotation which follows. The passage is taken from the Septuagint with the modification that the terms of the original, "all the tribes of the earth," are replaced by **all the nations,** (see Gen. xii. 3). They shall be blessed *in him* in the sense that their blessing (justification by faith), is typically included in his own. **In** here denotes to Paul the relation of spiritual sonship which is based on faith. Others understand the blessing more comprehensively (as Wieseler, De Wette) as referring to participation in the kingdom of God in general. **The Gentiles** (lit. the nations, τὰ ἔθνη) is here the contrast to the Jews. The same words in the original are found in the quotation where they have the same meaning. Perhaps the term, **the nations** (*i. e.* Gentiles, τὰ ἔθνη) was chosen in preference to "the tribes" (αἱ φυλαί) of the original,—which would certainly include Jews,—in order the more clearly to apply the passage to the heathen world. On this supposition, Paul uses the passage in a somewhat more specific sense than that which the original bears, in so far as he limits it by changing "tribes of the earth," including Jews, to "the nations," meaning Gentiles, thus suggesting a contrast of Gentiles to Jews. It is, however, at most, a specific limitation or application; not a change of the original force of the passage.

9. So then they which be of faith are blessed with the faithful Abraham.—This verse draws the conclusion from the confessed fact that the Galatian Christians received the Holy Spirit "by the hearing of faith," (vv. 2, 5); and asserts the harmony of this fact with the principle illustrated in the typical case of Abraham, and with the promise given to him. **With** gives the same fundamental conception as "in" (8) but with a different phase of thought. Together they would signify that *in* and *with* his blessing, they were blessed. The former implies the spiritual kinship which the latter more explicitly expresses.

10. For as many as are of the works of the law are under a curse: for it is written, Cursed is every one which continueth not in all things that are written in the book of the law, to do them.—The statements here made are the proof that the blessing of justification comes only by faith and are based upon the affirmation of Scripture that only a curse (and not a blessing) comes to those who adhere to the plane of mere law. In the phrase, **as many as are of works of the law, we have for the first time the exact counterpart of, "they which be of faith" (9). The citation here found is quoted freely, but without variation of sense, from the Septuagint (Deut. xxvii. 26), which, in turn, renders freely but not inexactly, the Old Testament "Cursed is he who does not maintain (יָקִים) the words of this law to do them." The contrast here intended is clearly stated in Rom. iv. 4, 5. The principle is stated positively in Rom. ii. 13; "The doers of a law shall be justified," and again in Rom. x. 5. The reason why *in fact* this doing of the law is never successful, *i. e.* never conducts to salvation, is found primarily in man's sinfulness which has its seat in the flesh (σάρξ) (*cf.* Rom. viii. 3). So far from justifying, it is found that the law can only produce the knowledge of sin and quicken the indwelling evil into new energy, but cannot deliver man from its power. (See especially Rom. iii. 20).

The assumption of the whole argument is that no one can perfectly keep the law, hence all **are** under its penalty. He who should render a complete and constant obedience could establish a meritorious claim to salvation; but there is no such person: "*Every one* is cursed who does not do *everything* which the law requires." Much of the emphasis and force of Paul's argumentative use of the passage depends upon the words **every one** and **all things,** which are, indeed, in the Septuagint (from which Paul's quotations are directly taken), but not in the original. They may have been in the text from which the translation of the Seventy was made. The force of the argument does not depend upon these emphases for which our Hebrew text supplies no basis, but it is plain that its force is greatly enhanced by them. The argument hinges also on the idea of *doing;* in legal relations *doing* is the test, but no one *does* the law, hence no one can be justified by it. Paul here gives to the passage from Deuteronomy (as in Rom. x. 5 to the passage from Lev. xviii. 5) a specific application which the passage in its original Old Testament setting did not bear, in using it so as to point a contrast between the law-principle and the faith-principle; between a debit and credit method and a gracious method of divine action. Both the passages just alluded to are general enforcements of the law-codes in which they occur. They were not meant to imply that everything which the people received from God should be in mathematical proportion to the degree of this obedience. Paul states with abstract exactness the legal principle, and treats it as a complete contrast to the gospel principle, but as a matter of fact the Old Testament did not present the principle to the Jews in this abstract character. There was to them a gospel in the law; the legal system was not merely abstractly legal, but gracious as well. Of course Paul does not say that it was so, but it cannot escape notice that he draws this contrast with a sharpness which, while abstractly exact, was never concretely illustrated in the Old Testament, and was not present to the minds of the writers of the passages referred to.

11, 12. Now that no man is justified by the law in the sight of God, is evident: for, The righteous shall live by faith, and the law is not of faith; but, He that doeth them shall live in them.— The argument of 11, 12 in syllogistic form would be: major premise, It is a Scripture axiom that the just man lives from faith: minor premise, But *doing* and *merit* are the test on the plane of law; therefore no one lives the just life **by the law** (ἐν νόμῳ). The underlying assumption of the argument is: No one perfectly keeps the law. The first quotation is from Hab. ii. 4 (צַדִּיק בֶּאֱמוּנָתוֹ יִחְיֶה). (LXX., ὁ δὲ δίκαιος ἐκ πίστεώς μου ζήσεται). The passage is quoted exactly from the Septuagint both here and in Rom. i. 17, except that the word "my" (μου) is omitted. The original passage is a part of the prophet's encouragement to the people in view of a Chaldean invasion. He declares that the destruction of the enemy is sure to come. "Be encouraged" he says, "and trust in Jehovah; the righteous man, the true Israelite, shall live by his constancy, fidelity" (אֱמוּנָה). Apart from the particular circumstances surrounding the passage, it becomes an assurance that the righteous man shall, in the exercise of faithfulness, find life and blessing. It is possible to join the phrase **by faith** with **shall live** (as is commonly done) or with **the righteous** (so Meyer). For the expression of the latter idea another order of words (ὁ ἐκ πίστεως δίκαιος) would have been unambiguous, but may have been prevented by the well-known order of words in the LXX. Whether it is the *righteousness* or the *life* which is said to be "from faith" makes no essential difference. The common connection is favored by the evident meaning of the original passage in the Old Testament. It is certain, however, that the word for faith here (πίστις) is more specific than the corresponding Hebrew term in the original passage. It is frequently rendered by the same Greek word (πίστις) in the LXX., and this usage is the connecting link between the more general Old Testament idea and Paul's specific conception of faith. As Abraham's faith was not exactly the same as the Christian's in content, yet was for Paul the same in principle, viz.: trust in God's grace, so the faithfulness in hardship and danger spoken of in Habakkuk is treated as being the same in principle with the specific faith which is exercised towards Christ for salvation. So the matter is treated, but we should not suppose that Paul turned his attention consciously to the limitation of the meaning in the Old Testament, and deliberately decided to use the passage in a somewhat different sense. He seized the words for the principle which they contained, and without reference to the Old Testament setting. The law does not spring out of the principle of faith, but out of a different principle, that of enactment and obedience. Hence, of course, we have nothing to hope from the law, and the conclusion is: **No man is justified by the law.** The Apostle evidently intends to prove this by the Old Testament quotations, so that the Jewish party will be powerless to reply. He has put two passages of Scripture together as premises, and drawn his conclusion. So long as they accept these Scriptures they must accept his conclusion unless they should dispute his use of the passages.*

---

* What flaw would a keen scribe be likely to have found here from his viewpoint? Perhaps in reference to the first quotation he would object that "faith" in the passage means constancy and fidelity to God and would maintain that the prophet's view and his own were the same, viz.: that a man shall live now as then by fidelity to

13. Christ redeemed us from the curse of the law, having become a curse for us: for it is written, Cursed is every one that hangeth on a tree.—In verses 11 and 12 Paul had shown that under the law, not a blessing, but a curse, is experienced. Through Christ the curse is taken away. This process is represented by commercial analogies. The curse is conceived as a debt to be met. God as the lawgiver exacted obedience; it has not been rendered; there is an unpaid obligation which puts men in a relation to

---

God. He might urge that " faith " in the Old Testament passage does not bear the sense of *trust* as opposed to legal obedience and hold that he supported the principle precisely in its Old Testament sense. Perhaps in regard to the second quotation he would say that " shall live" does not refer to justification, and that the passage is not meant to establish an exact relation under the Old Testament between *doing* and *receiving from God;* that it means rather that the man who is obedient in heart and purpose shall have life, room being left for gracious forgiveness for sins and failures. He might conclude:—" We hold both these principles too, but in the sense in which they stand in the Old Testament, and in that sense they have no bearing upon specific faith in Christ." Paul might answer: " The passages bear on the two *principles* which are the conspicuous marks of the two systems respectively. They show that from the Old Testament itself it was clear that salvation is not by debt but of grace; *i. e.* that, even under the Old Testament, justification by faith was the principle of salvation, as illustrated by the case of Abraham ".

God which might be likened to that of captives, who, having been false to their rightful king, are held awaiting ransom. Christ pays that ransom and the obligation arising from the violated law is forever discharged. His death for men is the ransom price. He becomes a curse; *i. e.* he vicariously takes the place of those whom he sets free, enduring the penal sufferings which must have been theirs under the curse of the law. *Cf.* II Cor. v. 21, where Christ is said to become "sin for us."

Next the idea of the curse under which Christ, as the Redeemer, comes, is enforced by the Old Testament statement (Deut. xxi. 23) of the ignominy attaching to such as have their bodies hung upon a stake or tree. So far did Christ become as one accursed that he stopped not short of this pitch of shame. Respecting the theological bearing of these statements it may be observed, (*a*) that Paul is not presenting an abstract theory of the mode of redemption. The pronoun "us" ("redeemed us") refers primarily to the Jews who alone were under the Mosaic law. It is neither of law in the abstract nor of man in the abstract, that Paul is speaking. He is not speculating as to how Christ's vicarious sufferings satisfy the penal righteousness of God; although theological speculation, following out his language, must face this question. He is treating a concrete question: the way in which Christ helped the Jews out of that bondage of debt which their disobedience involved them in.

(*b*) It is to be remembered that **the** (Mosaic) **law** with Paul is only *one* of the dispensations of God. There was also the gracious covenant of promise which antedates the law, (verses 17-19). This dispensation is the older and more fundamental; the law entered alongside (παρεισῆλθεν, Rom. v. 20) of it four hundred and twenty years after to make transgressions abound, and thus led on to the ideal fulfillment of the covenant of promise whose principle is faith (*cf.* Rom. iv. 13-16). The law and this primeval gospel existed side by side, and the law must by no means be conceived of as annulling that gospel of promise (v. 21). The Mosaic law represents but one phase of the divine economy, and that a subordinate one; the gospel of grace and faith antedates it, and contains the higher ends which it is to serve. Thus there existed a gospel of God's grace according to which he was forgiving men upon faith, before the law, alongside of the law, and after the law is done away. The whole purpose of the law is subordinate to God's gracious redemption; it comes in to reveal the exceeding sinfulness of sin, for this is a necessary step in the redemption of man from it. It follows that redemption is not conceived of as a makeshift to satisfy the law, but as the product of divine ideas and modes of action that are more fundamental and original than the legal system. While Christ satisfies the demands of the law for obedience, the larger Pauline truth is, that he satisfies the ends to which the legal system, first, midst and last, is subordinate.

(c) It is important for theology to translate the figure of ransoming into its moral and spiritual equivalents and to build on these, not on the form or metaphor merely. The Mosaic law may be said to represent the law and penalty side of the divine nature; there is such a side. The primeval gospel of grace and faith may be said to represent the gracious, benevolent element in the nature of God. Both of these are constituent in the divine nature. Both must be manifested, revealed, satisfied, by any divine method or process of salvation. Christ, in his vicarious identification of himself with man in his sinful condition, comes into the intense realization of the misery and hatefulness to God, of human sin. He suffers with and for man by virtue of his union with him in his sinful lot. In this sense he becomes **a curse** or "sin," for us. His sufferings are penal, not in the sense that they are personally deserved, nor that he comes under the personal displeasure of God; but in the sense that just so far as he is identified with man through the vicariousness of love, he is identified with him in suffering the consequences of sin. The severity of this suffering freely borne by the sinless Christ is the vindication of God's attitude towards sin. Christ must suffer as he does, because he has become the representative man, and those sufferings are the answer to the question: What is God's feeling toward sin?

In Christ's sufferings there is therefore a revelation of the holy nature of God which vindicates that holiness beyond what punishment could do. Thus Christ meets the ends of punishment. This is the essential truth underlying the figure of the ransom. The act or process denoted by this term is vicarious, but the vicariousness is moral and spiritual; there is, indeed, no other vicariousness, which is of any value.

14. That upon the Gentiles might come the blessing of Abraham in Christ Jesus; that we might receive the promise of the Spirit through faith.—This verse states the purpose or aim of the redemption of the Jews from the curse, as terminating on the Gentiles. How should the deliverance of the Jews from the curse which the law pronounced secure justification (**the blessing of Abraham**) to the Gentiles? Various replies are given:

(1) Christ does away with the Jewish law, and breaks down the partition between Jew and Gentile (Rückert, Lightfoot). But Paul says nothing of doing away with the law here, but only of ransoming men from its curse. This view seems to be influenced by Eph. ii. 14, ff.

(2) Christ redeems the Jews from the curse, thereby putting Jew and Gentile on one common ground, in that he requires faith alike in both (Usteri). But this would not yet show how the redemption of the Jews accomplished the justification of the Gentiles.

(3) The Jews were the divinely chosen media through whom salvation should be brought to the Gentiles. "Salvation is of the Jews." Their redemption logically precedes the salvation of the Gentiles, on the principle: "To the Jew first," etc. (Meyer). This interpretation is the preferable one. This blessing is to come to the Gentiles **in Christ Jesus,** as opposed to "through the law." The second final clause, **that we might receive,** etc., may be taken as co-ordinate with the first, **that upon the Gentiles,** etc., by way of climax (so Meyer, Ellicott); or as subordinate to the first as further defining it (Lightfoot). Either construction makes good sense.

THE PRINCIPLE OF THE GOSPEL ANTEDATES AND UNDERLIES THE LAW, 15-22.

15. Brethren, I speak after the manner of men: Though it be but a man's covenant, yet when it hath been confirmed, no one maketh it void, or addeth thereto.
—Here begins the argument to show the priority and superiority of the covenant of promise with

Abraham to which the law was subordinate. **After the manner of men** (κατὰ ἄνθρωπον), means, "in accordance with what happens among men." It introduces an argument *a fortiori* to show that, if a covenant, properly ratified, is certain in human relations, much more will a divine promise be secure. **Covenant** (διαθήκη) is the equivalent of the Old Testament term (בְּרִית), and signifies a solemn compact or agreement. It means "testament" or "will," only once in the New Testament (Heb. ix. 16, 17)—a meaning common in classic Greek,—but being translated *testamentum* by the Vulgate, the rendering "testament" has passed into our common usage as its English equivalent. Of this inaccuracy the title "The New Testament" must now stand as a perpetual witness. The correct title would have been "The New Covenant." In the text the R. V. has set the translation right. **Addeth thereto** (ἐπιδιατάσσεται), *i. e.* "to ordain besides," "to add stipulations to." The word translated **yet** (ὅμως) belongs logically with **no one** (οὐδείς), though separated so far from it, in the original text, (*cf.* I Cor. xiv. 7); the participle (κεκυρωμένην) is temporal: "when confirmed." The object of the sentence, **a man's covenant,** is thrown into the emphatic position, and the particular emphasis is like that given by a concessive clause: "Even though it be the case of a human covenant, yet, when it is confirmed, no one," etc., or, "Man's covenant though it be, yet," etc. The confirmation spoken of is the solemn ratification of the agreement by the contracting parties. When this is done no one (*i. e.* no third party) sets it aside or adds to it. It must stand, so far as any outside interference is concerned. This he will now apply. The typical covenant-promise is to Abraham. It is confirmed by God; and no one (such as a Judaizer, or an adherent of the Mosaic law), must interfere with or replace its provisions.

16. Now to Abraham were the promises spoken, and to his seed. He saith not, And to seeds, as of many; but as of one, And to thy seed, which is Christ.— The truth which he now wishes to establish is the indestructible character of the Abrahamic covenant and its connection with Christ. **The promises,** —the plural denoting that they were oft repeated, and in different forms,—were spoken to Abraham; but also to his seed. They were not merely spoken personally to Abraham, but had a forward look which Paul associates with Christ. The quotation includes the connecting word **and.** The words are found in Gen. xiii. 15 and xvii. 8. And he saith not: **And to seeds** (καὶ τοῖς σπέρμασιν), as if referring to many, but: **And to thy seed** (καὶ τῷ σπέρματί σου), as if referring to one, who is Christ.

The various methods of explaining this difficult passage may be summarized thus: (*a*) The object of

Paul is to show that the promise referred to does not apply to Abraham's descendants in a literal sense, but to one class of his descendants, his spiritual children (so Augustine, Tholuck, Olshausen; similarly, Ellicott, Lightfoot). Of this spiritual progeny of Abraham, Christ is the head; indeed it has no existence apart from Christ. It is he in a mystical sense. (*b*) The argument with Paul turns on the use in the Old Testament of the singular number and not the plural (σπέρμα, not σπέρματα). His meaning is: since the singular is used, the passage proves that one individual must be referred to, and that must be Christ. The passage cannot refer to many descendants of Abraham, but must refer to one, that anti-typical Son of Abraham, who has the closest spiritual relationship with Abraham, the man of faith, viz.: Christ. In the original, however, the word for seed (זרע) is a collective noun, as it regularly is in the Old Testament in such cases. (So Meyer, Weiss and German critics generally). There is, I think, a truth in both views, which must be recognized. *Formaliter*, the latter view is more nearly correct; *materialiter*, the former. Paul's method of argument is undoubtedly Rabbinic, and he draws more from the use of the singular than an exact exegesis of the Old Testament can directly justify, but not more than according to the typical view of prophecy which is pervading in the New Testament, can be justly claimed to be *involved* in the passage. The essential idea is: The promise to Abraham meets its true, ideal fulfillment only in Christ. The argument, if formally unwarranted, rests nevertheless on the profound view of Old Testament prophecy and history as looking forward to Christ, and reaching its culmination only in him. Wieseler justly says (Com. *in loco*): "That the idea of the Messiah is veiled in the Abrahamic promise, and that we may understand the expression 'seed of Abraham' in the light of later revelation to refer really to the Messiah, is the thoroughly correct view upon which the whole explanation of Paul rests, but the form in which he incidentally expresses this correct view in this passage is due to his Rabbinic training." It is to be remembered that Paul's argument by no means rests upon this particular interpretation. Speaking on this point, Luther quaintly and aptly says that this argument is but the painting of the house which has been already built.

17. Now this I say; A covenant confirmed beforehand by God, the law, which came four hundred and thirty years after, doth not disannul, so as to make the promise of none effect.—Now follows the application of what was said in verse 15. No third party can break up or add to a covenant between two parties. Now the law, if it interfered with the covenant of promise, which pointed to Christ, would be doing that. But that it cannot do, especially since God is a party to the transaction. This covenant has faith as its human condition. It is a kind of divine ratification beforehand of the faith-principle, and especially so because it is Messianic. The faith-principle is older and more fundamental than the law system. The law came in long after,—four hundred and thirty years (Exod. xii. 40). In Gen. xv. 13 and Acts vii. 6 it is the round number four hundred. In the LXX. at Ex. xii. 40 the sojourn in Egypt and Canaan is said to be four hundred and thirty years. This reckoning is found in Josephus and elsewhere, and would materially shorten the sojourn in Egypt. Opinion is divided as to which is the more correct. Paul's statement harmonizes with the LXX., in which four hundred and thirty embraces the time from Abraham's call to the Exodus, but is against the Old Testament Hebrew text, as we have it, and against Acts vii. 6, where four hundred and thirty embraces only the Egyptian period.

18. For if the inheritance is of the law it is no more of promise; but God hath granted it to Abraham by promise.—This verse marks the opposition to which the argument has been leading up, **the inheritance** ($\dot{\eta}$ $\kappa\lambda\eta\rho o\nu o\mu\acute{\iota}a$) of the Messianic blessing must come either in the line of the law or of promise (implying grace and faith).

The two are mutually exclusive. If the inheritance is in the line of the gracious promise, which has been made on condition of faith, and only so, then it cannot be of the law (ἐκ νόμου). And the Scriptural argument has plainly shown that the former is the case, the latter possibility is therefore excluded. Note the way in which the gospel (promise, faith, etc.,) is brought up in contrast with the law in Galatians, a result of the Judaizing attachment to the covenant which Paul is combating. It is enough in Romans to show that faith has always been the way of salvation and that sinfulness prevents the practicability of justification by works. But here the two must be sharply *contrasted* and their mutual exclusiveness shown. When one now adheres to the law he is opposing the original divine covenant; setting himself against the primeval way of salvation, and the deepest principle of the divine procedure. The law came in only as a temporary expedient, a "tutor unto Christ" (v. 24). It has no equal rights with the promise. It is treated, when such a claim is made for it, as an interfering party seeking to break up a sealed contract or to get a codicil inserted into a will in favor of itself. It serves a good but temporary end. Now that faith is come we are no longer under the provisional tutor (παιδαγωγός).

19. What then is the law? It was added because of transgressions, till the seed should come to whom the promise

hath been made ; and it was ordained through angels by the hand of a mediator.—Having now shown that the promise antedates the law, and that the inheritance of Messianic blessings is connected with the promise, and not with the law, the question arises what were the purpose and use of the law? Paul answers: **It was added because of trangressions** (τῶν παραβάσεων χάριν προσετέθη). To these words three interpretations are given: (1) To check transgressions (so Olshausen, Neander). This view is against the context, and the Pauline doctrine, *cf.* especially Rom. v. 20. (2) That men might recognize their transgressions (so Augustine, Calvin, Ellicott). This interpretation proceeds in the right direction, but does not fully express the Pauline view of the function of the law. (3) To multiply transgressions. The law reveals, provokes, and multiplies transgressions (Rom. iii. 20; vii. 7; v. 20). "Where there is no law there is no transgression (παράβασις), (Rom. iv. 15). There is *sin* (ἁμαρτία) but not *transgression*. The purpose of the law is to bring out sin into definite expression as transgression (so Lightfoot, Meyer). Thus sin is revealed to itself, its ill desert is seen, the displeasure of God is felt, and the sinner sees himself as guilty and punishable. This knowledge leads him to seek salvation. Meyer says: "The real idea of the Apostle is that the emergence of sins, viz., in the penal wrath-deserving moral form of *transgressions*, which the law brought about was designed by God (who must indeed have foreseen this effect), when he gave the law, and designed in fact as a mediate end in reference to the future redemption; for the evil was to become truly great that it might nevertheless be outdone by grace" (Rom. v. 20). Paul holds that what the law did it was intended to do. Does it then increase sin and was this its purpose? Not in the sense of enhancing the amount of moral evil in the world, but in the sense of bringing out this evil into the form of conscious transgression where it can be seen and felt, and therefore forsaken. The law provokes in this sin a reaction against itself, and it bursts into expression and activity, but its principle was there before. The sin was not created by the the law, but only its expression, (transgression), was caused or stimulated by the law. **Was added** ($\pi\rho o\sigma\epsilon\tau\acute{\epsilon}\theta\eta$) indicates that the law was something supplementary to the promise. *Cf.* "Came in beside" ($\pi\alpha\rho\epsilon\iota\sigma\tilde{\eta}\lambda\theta\epsilon\nu$, Rom. v. 20). It holds a secondary rank compared with the promise. **The seed** ($\tau\grave{o}$ $\sigma\pi\acute{\epsilon}\rho\mu\alpha$) here refers to Christ, (*cf.* verse 16). **To whom the promise hath been made** ($\epsilon\pi\acute{\eta}\gamma\gamma\epsilon\lambda\tau\alpha\iota$); the perfect tense denotes the past and abiding fact of the confirmed promise. **Ordained through angels** ($\delta\iota\alpha\tau\alpha\gamma\epsilon\grave{\iota}\varsigma$ $\delta\iota'$ $\dot{\alpha}\gamma\gamma\acute{\epsilon}\lambda\omega\nu$); the law was ordained through the mediation of angels, and was entrusted to a mediator, Moses. The reference to the mediation of angels in the giving of the law is found in the LXX. rendering of Deut. xxxiii. 2. The original passage is uncertain in meaning, since there is doubt regarding the pointing of a word which in our text signifies "Holiness" (קֹדֶשׁ): hence, "myriads of holiness." Some, however, interpret this word to mean Kadesh, (and indeed so the LXX. but they also add the reference to angels, which must, therefore, have been found in the text used by them). Rabbinical literature greatly elaborated this idea of angel mediation; it is also found in Heb. ii. 2.

By the hand ($\dot{\epsilon}\nu$ $\chi\epsilon\iota\rho\dot{\iota}$) may be taken literally (so Meyer) as a reference to Moses receiving the tables of the law; or understood as a Hebraism (בְּיַד). **Mediator,** ($\mu\epsilon\sigma\iota\tau\eta\varsigma$), that is, Moses, and not Christ, (as the Church Fathers usually understood it), an interpretation which would confuse the argument. Is this introduction of angels and Moses designed to depreciate the law as compared with the promise (as most critics maintain), or to exalt the promise by showing that such a glorious system as the law was auxiliary to it? (So Meyer, Winer, Wieseler). *Cf.*, in this connection, the argument in Heb. ii. 1–4. Which is more directly appropriate to the Apostle's course of thought in our passage, a glorifying, or a relative depreciation of the law? I think the latter.

20. Now a mediator is not a mediator of one; but God is one.—The connection of thought may be indicated thus: In the case of the giving of the law there was a mediator, Moses. That implied something of the nature of a contract, because a mediator involves two parties; God was one party and the people of Israel the other. The law-system therefore, might be terminated whenever the relations of the parties might require it. It was relative and conditional. But in the case of the promise there was no mediator; that is, it was an act of God alone and was absolute and unconditional. The promise was a sovereign declaration proceeding from God and extending to all time. It therefore stands upon a higher plane than this mediated and conditional system. The sense of the words, therefore is: "Now a mediator implies two parties, but God (in making the promise) is one, that is, stands alone and is sovereign in his action." Hence the implied conclusion: The promise has an absolute character, as compared with the contingent law-system, and thus stands above it.

21. Is the law then against the promises of God? God forbid: for if there had been a law given which could make alive, verily righteousness would have been of the law.—But now, the question arises: If the law and the promise stand on different planes, shall we go further and say that they are in antagonism?

No, answers the Apostle, and why? Because they serve different ends and cannot be compared. Those things cannot be said to be in antagonism which do not come into competition at all. If the law ever could have saved men, then an antagonism might, perhaps, be spoken of, but since it could not do this, it could not be said to be a rival system to the promise. The full reason for Paul's denial of such a conclusion (μὴ γένοιτο) is contained in the whole passage, vv. 21-24, and may be summarized thus: "If there had ever been any law which could have given life, then righteousness might have been attained by means of it, and that law would have been a rival of the promise; but, as a matter of fact, the Mosaic law, so far from giving life, pronounces a curse, shuts men up under sin as if in prison, and holds them there in ward, until the promise comes and delivers them. Thus the immediate aim of the law is not to procure salvation, but only to make men conscious of their need of Christ, by showing them their guilt. The law thus has its purpose as subordinate to the gospel, and hence can never be against it or come into rivalry with it."

22. Howbeit the scripture hath shut up all things under sin, that the promise by faith in Jesus Christ might be given to them that believe.—This verse points the contrast between such a case as is supposed in v. 21, and the actual case of the Mosaic law. Paul cites the testimony of the Old Testament in regard to what the Mosaic law does. **The scripture** (personified) **hath shut up all things under sin;** *i. e.* by showing men how sinful they were, it kept them shut up as under a charge of guilt until the time of the Messianic deliverance. **All things** (τὰ πάντα) is the neuter plural of category referring to persons, (*cf.* I Cor. i. 27, 28). But this custody was not for its own sake, but as a necessary step toward the final fulfillment of the gracious promise. The purpose is stated in the clause beginning **that the promise,** etc. **Promise** (ἐπαγγελία) is here equivalent to the fulfillment of the promise (*i. e.*, of course, justification) as the verb **might be given** (δοθῇ) shows. The idea of faith being the condition of receiving this promise is twice stated in the phrases **by faith** (ἐκ πίστεως) and **them that believe** (τοῖς πιστεύουσιν), very probably because Paul is not content to say that it is given to believers (which all would allow), but wishes to especially emphasize the idea that it is given them **by faith** (emphatic) and not also "by works," as the Judaizing Christians would suppose.

III. THE DISCIPLINARY AND PREPARATORY OFFICE OF THE LAW, 23-29.

23. But before faith came, we were kept in ward under the law, shut up unto the faith which should afterwards be re-

vealed:—**Faith** is here half personified (*cf.* the predicate **came**) and objectively treated, but without ceasing to mean subjective faith in Christ. The thought is : " Before the gospel whose characteristic is faith, came," etc. **We were kept in ward** (ἐφρουρούμεθα), *i. e.*, We (Jews) were kept in ward by the law (personified) as disobedient slaves are shut up in prison by their master ; **shut up unto** *i. e.* until the coming (for our deliverance) of the faith about to be revealed. The law did its utmost when it imprisoned us. It must wait for faith to come and open the door. **Unto** (εἰς) denotes the end contemplated in the action of shutting up ; it was that (by exercising faith) we might be released.

24. So that the law hath been our tutor to bring us unto Christ, that we might be justified by faith.—This statement concludes the description of the function of the law and sums up all that has been said concerning it. It " has become " (γέγονεν) in the divine providence our **tutor unto Christ** (παιδ. εἰς Χριστόν). This phrase has often been understood thus: As the pedagogue (generally a slave) in ancient times conducted the boy to school, so the law conducts us to the school of Christ, that we may learn of him (so Chrysostom, Erasmus). But this hangs too much on the word " pedagogue " or tutor, to the neglect of the context. The thought rather is that the law trained and disciplined the Jews for Christianity. Nor is the idea here that the law restrained from sin, and so was a preparation for Christ; but the reference is to that harsh treatment which the law administers to sinful men which constitutes its pedagogic function, its pronouncing of a curse upon them, and shutting them up under accusation, (so Meyer, Lightfoot and most moderns). The method of this discipline is sketched in Rom. vii. It prepares men for Christ because it begets dissatisfaction with themselves, reveals their sins, and (as Luther says) " humbles the proud to desire Christ's aid." On the force of the phrase **unto Christ,** Luther quaintly says: "For what a schoolmaster were he which would always torment and beat the child and teach him nothing at all? And yet, such schoolmasters there were in time past when schools were nothing else but a prison and a very hell, and the schoolmasters cruel tyrants and very butchers. The children were always beaten, they learned with continual pain and travail, and yet few of them came to any proof. The law is not such a schoolmaster. For it doth not only terrify and torment, as the foolish schoolmaster beateth his scholars and teacheth them nothing, but with his rods he driveth us unto Christ, like as a good schoolmaster instructeth and exerciseth his scholars in reading and writing, to the end that they may come to the knowledge of good letters and other profitable things, that afterwards they may have a delight in doing of that which before, when they were constrained thereunto, they did against their wills " (Commentary *in loco*).

Again Luther pithily says: "Therefore the law doth not only kill, but it killeth that we may live."

25. But now that faith is come, we are no longer under a tutor.—Since the law had it as its purpose to usher in the faith-system, it follows that, when that system enters, the law ceases to be in effect. **Faith** is here also objectively treated and almost personified, but still meaning, not primarily a doctrine, but an act of trust. **We** designates primarily Jews who had been under the tutor. The Gentiles, of course, had never been under the law.

26. For ye are all sons of God, through faith, in Christ Jesus.—The assurance, that the Jews are no longer under the tutor, the Apostle grounds by the general statement that the Galatian Christians, whether Jews or Gentiles, are sons of God. How should sonship to God prove that Christians are not under the law? Because, in the Apostle's view, the state under the law is a bondage in which men are servants (δοῦλοι), and not sons (υἱοί). The adoption (υἱοθεσία) brings in "the liberty of the glory of the children of God" (Rom. viii. 14, 15 *seq*.). Hence to be **sons of God** is to be free from the law, to enjoy the sense of pardon and of liberty from all that bondage and guilt which the law engenders. **Ye,** Galatian Christians, are *all* (emphatic position) such. The primary emphasis is on **all** as embracing Christians without distinction; and the secondary on **sons of God** as the contrast to the servitude "under a tutor." The phrase: **In Christ Jesus,** may be taken either with **ye are** or with the word **faith.** The construction of the preposition here used ($\dot{\epsilon}\nu$) after the words "faith" ($\pi i \sigma \tau \iota \varsigma$) or believing ($\pi \iota \sigma \tau \epsilon \dot{\upsilon} \epsilon \iota \nu$) occurs only in Mark i. 15; Eph. i. 13. It may be said, on the one hand, that taken with "faith" it is superfluous, because the meaning of "faith" is evident; to which it may be answered, that it adds a full and solemn emphasis to the meaning of the faith which is set in contrast to the law. The R. V. favors the former (so Lightfoot, Wieseler); the A. V. favors the latter (so Meyer and Ellicott); I prefer the latter construction.

27. For as many of you as were baptized into Christ did put on Christ.—The Apostle now explains the nature of this relation of sonship and faith: "Why do I insist that all you Christians are sons of God, entitled to the liberty and joy of sonship? I do so because all you who have been baptized, have entered into this deep and close union with Christ which constitutes your freedom and your salvation. So great things can be predicated of faith because it has brought you into such vital communion with Christ."

To be **baptized into Christ** (βαπ. εἰς Χριστόν) means to enter by baptism into the relationship of fellowship with Christ. Baptism is here expressly treated from the standpoint of the faith which it presupposes. The statement is introduced as an explanation of the sonship to God which arises on condition of faith. The statement is practically equivalent to: as many as have believed have entered into a spiritual union with Christ. (*Cf.* Rom. vi. 3). The figure of "putting on Christ" is very probably derived from the putting on of clothing, which comes to be applied to the taking on of qualities such as righteousness, shame, etc. In the Apostle's language it expresses the mystical union into which the believer enters with Christ at his conversion. Christ becomes, as it were, the life-element of the soul; Christ is in the believer, he is in Christ, his life is hid with Christ in God. He has put on Christ, entered into fellowship of life with him, so that in his relations to Christ are found the deepest meanings of his life.

28. There can be neither Jew nor Greek, there can be neither bond nor free, there can be no male and female; for ye all are one man in Christ Jesus. —Since this freedom and sonship are shared by all Christians by virtue of their common relation to Christ, it follows that there is among them a union deeper than diversities of nation, condition or sex.

The student of the original text will notice that while the relation of Jew and Greek, and of bond and free, are contrasted by the emphatic negative (οὐδέ), the terms male and female are connected by **and** (καί), indicating the difference of this distinction from those social ones mentioned above. The meaning of the verse is not, that Christianity knows no such distinctions in themselves, but that Christianity knows no such distinctions as essential or determining. It goes beneath and behind all these natural diversities and lays a deep ground for unity beneath them. The thought is: So far as any of these distinctions have ever been grounds of separation and estrangement among mankind, they are now non-existent, for those who breathe the one spirit which emanates from Christ.

29. And if ye are Christ's then are ye Abraham's seed, heirs according to promise.—If ye belong to Christ who is pre-eminently the **seed** of Abraham, then are ye also his **seed**, that is, true spiritual descendants of Abraham. Not those who are in lineal descent from Abraham and who make their boast in the law, but those who, like Abraham, exercise faith, are his true spiritual sons. They are like him, walk in his footsteps, and illustrate that which was most characteristic and significant in his life. The believers, then, are the true inheritors of the Messianic salvation. This is said in opposition to the Apostle's Judaizing opponents, who made heirship to depend also upon observance of the law. The great terms of the discussion thus far are, according to Paul's system, on the divine side, "promise" (ἐπαγγελία); on the human side "faith" (πίστις). Result, in the former case, "inheritance" (κληρονομία) or "righteousness" (δικαιοσύνη); the correlative terms in the view opposed by the Apostle are, on the divine side, "the law" (ὁ νόμος); on the human, "works" (ἔργα νόμου), and the result a "curse" (κατάρα).

ANALYSIS AND PARAPHRASE OF CHAPTER IV.

1. *Our position under the law and under the Gospel,* 1–7.—The heir, before he attains his majority, can no more enter upon the actual possession of his destined estate, than can a bond servant in the family possess himself of it (1). Until the set time, he must continue in a subordinate position, under the authority and discipline of others (2). Our position (he is here thinking more particularly of the Jewish Christians) under the law was analogous. We were as children, having a great inheritance (the gospel) in prospect, but kept in a preparatory process of training (3), but the coming of Christ marks the period of release from this tutelage and of entrance upon the promised possession (4, 5). This full sense of sonship is imparted by the testimony of the Holy Spirit to the heart of the believer, assuring him of the divine fatherhood (6); hence we are no longer in the position of servants, but in that of the sons of full age in the family who have attained the clear consciousness of

sonship and with it have entered upon their rightful, destined possession.

2. *The stage of religious development represented by the law,* 8–11.—(He is speaking now more particularly with reference to the Gentile Christians). We were all in bondage before we became Christians, either to the law, or under a worse master, idolatry (8); but since we have through Christ learned to know the true and only God, or rather, since he has made himself known to us, how unreasonable in us to wish to return to an elementary stage of religion again, by continuing to adhere to the Jewish observances. That is like going back to bondage after having been once set free (9). This you Galatians are doing; your observances of Jewish feast-days and ceremonies, make me afraid that my labor among you will prove to have been for naught (10, 11).

3. *Exhortation to the Galatians to return to the true Christian position,* 12–20.—Let me plead with you to come to my point of view in this matter, even as I, in renouncing Judaism, put myself upon the same plane with you Gentiles (12). I hope for this result from my experience of your former kindness and attachment, for I remember that when I was detained among you by sickness, in consequence of which I became your Christian teacher, you did not consider my presence among you burdensome, nor did your regard fail to endure the test to which

Analysis and Paraphrase of Chapter IV. 153

it was put; on the contrary, you received me with the utmost,—indeed, with excessive honor (13, 14). But all seems changed now! You appear not to count it any felicity now to receive and obey my instructions. How great the change of temper, for when I was among you, you would gladly have made the greatest sacrifice for me (15). Have I become the object of your enmity because I now urge upon you the true and only gospel (16)?

Those who are leading you astray from my teaching (the Judaizing leaders) are indeed eager in courting your favor, but it is in no good spirit and for no good end; what they really seek is to impart to you an exclusive and partisan spirit (*cf.* notes), that they may attach you to themselves as followers and supporters (17). It is always well to be zealously sought after by others if the object of this enthusiasm is a worthy one. I do not begrudge you this attention from others; when I am absent others must exercise this care (*cf.* notes), (18). My children, so great is my anxiety for you on account of your defection from the truth that I seem to be again undergoing the pains and labors by which you were brought into the church. I should be glad to be personally present with you and to adopt a less censorious tone; for I am perplexed and uncertain whether I can by any means win you back and would gladly make all possible efforts (19, 20).

4. *A narrative from the law itself may be allegor-*

ically applied so as to illustrate the truth that those who adhere to the law are in bondage, 21–v. 1.—My readers who are familiar with the Old Testament will readily recall the history of Abraham's two sons, Ishmael and Isaac, the former the child of the bondwoman, Hagar, whose birth was merely in the ordinary course of nature, and Isaac, the child of Sarah, born in accordance with a divine promise (21–23). These persons and events have an allegorical significance. The two women, Hagar and Sarah, represent respectively the Old and the New Testament systems; the former—the bondwoman— corresponds to the covenant whose sign or symbol is Mt. Sinai, since her children, like those who continue under the Old Covenant, are brought forth in and for a state of bondage (24). Now this analogy is the more appropriate because Mt. Sinai is actually situated in Arabia, the land of Hagar's descendants (so R. V. *margin; cf.* notes).* If, then, Hagar fitly represents Sinai, she may as fitly be said to represent the earthly city of Jerusalem, which stands as a symbol of the Jewish religion. Sinai and Jerusalem have the same religious significance. Jerusalem (personified as the mother of the Jewish people), like Hagar and her descendants, is in

---

* Following the text of the R. V. the analysis would be: Now the correspondence between Hagar and Sinai is seen in the fact that the name Hagar is applied to the mountain by the people of Arabia, etc.

Analysis and Paraphrase of Chapter IV. 155

bondage with her children (25). But the upper Jerusalem, the spiritual commonwealth, typified by Sarah, is free and, since she is the mother of all believers, her children (Christians) are also free (26). Our spiritual mother may rejoice, therefore, in the language of ancient prophecy concerning the hope of the childless, and we, her children, like Isaac, are heirs of God's gracious promise, made to all believers (27, 28).

But as in ancient days, so now, the spiritual must suffer persecution from the unspiritual (29). But as then, the Ishmaelites were rejected from the true theocracy, so now shall the unfree Jews who persist in refusing their spiritual freedom in Christ, be excluded from the people of God (30). We are free then; let us maintain and prize our freedom and not surrender it by returning to the bondage with which the law enslaves those who try to be saved by its works (21, v. 1).

CHAPTER IV.

I. OUR POSITION UNDER THE LAW AND UNDER THE GOSPEL, 1-7.

1. But I say that so long as the heir is a child, he differeth nothing from a bondservant, though he is lord of all.—This verse explains that even the one who is the destined heir in the family, must continue for a time without entering upon his possession. Until he is of age he cannot inherit, but remains, so far as possession in his own right is concerned, on the same plane with a servant in the family. Instead of being master he is more in the position of a servant (δοῦλος), so long as he is under age (νήπιος).

2. But is under guardians and stewards until the term appointed of the father.— He is under guardians, overseers (ἐπίτροποι) and stewards (οἰκονόμοι) who exercise authority over him and discipline him, notwithstanding his destined superiority. Now we Jews, continues the Apostle in v. 3, were in this case. We were destined to possess the Messianic inheritance, but not before the time. There was a period of our minority when we must stand on the plane of servants and receive tutelage and chastisement. That was the law-period, and the law was the disciplinarian. This was the period of waiting and training. But now the time of our majority is come. We should enter into our divinely destined inheritance. **Child** (*νήπιος*) may mean either a babe, or a legal minor (as here). Commonly in Paul's writings it is opposed to a mature, full-grown man (*τέλειος*). Here it is practically so, but the contrast is not explicitly made, because the Apostle changes the figure of minority vs. majority, and shades off into that of servitude and sonship, in verse 5 *seq.*

Differeth nothing from (*οὐδὲν διαφέρει*), *i. e.* so far as the necessity of discipline and training is concerned. He is indeed prospective master but must in his youth be governed and trained by others, just as much as if he were the child of a bondservant in the family. **Though he is lord of all,** "Lord of all in prospect though he is." During his nonage he is under **guardians** or overseers, who have charge of his education, and **stewards,** who have the management of the property which he will inherit, until the **term appointed** (*ἀχρι τῆς προθεσμίας—sc. ἡμέρας—τοῦ πατρός*); the time which must elapse before the attainment of full age is here spoken of as being determined by the father. In both Jewish and Roman law the age at which majority was reached was determined by statute; but Paul was in no way concerned with the technical arrangements on this point. It serves better as an illustration to speak of the father as determining the time, which indeed he could do so far as to put an end to the tutelage under which he chose to have his child trained. The question is sometimes raised whether the father is conceived of as living? It is irrelevant to Paul's argument. Does the "we" (v. 3) refer to the Jews (Wieseler) or to all Christians (Meyer)? The answer must be: Strictly, to the Jews who alone were under the tutelage of the law, and the servitude connected therewith, though the same principles might be equally well applied, with change of terms, to the pre-Christian Gentile world who possessed an analogue to the Mosaic law, the revelation of God in nature and conscience. (Rom. i. 18–23).

3. So we also, when we were children, were held in bondage under the rudiments of the world.—We (Jews) were in our pre-Christian state enslaved **under the rudiments of the world** (τὰ στοιχεῖα τοῦ κόσμου); evidently a designation for the law. What does it mean? The same expression is found in Col. ii. 8 and 20, "If ye died with Christ to the rudiments of the world," why do ye, as living (in a pre-Christian state), subject yourselves to such ascetic rules as "touch not, taste not, handle not," etc.? Hence these ascetic abstinences (δόγματα), are examples of the rudiments of the world spoken of. In Gal. iv. 9, where those who are heathen are addressed, we have the term **rudiments** (στοιχεῖα) used of Jewish observances to which the Galatians were inclined to turn, and, by clear implication, used to characterize their former idolatrous worship. The expression may, therefore, refer to those elementary and imperfect religious devotions and observances, whether Jewish or heathen, which preceded Christianity. The same word is applied in Heb. v. 12 to the elements of Christian doctrine.

These observances and services of imperfect religions are rudiments in so far as they represent only an imperfect state of religious knowledge. They belong to the **world** (κόσμος), as being outward and visible, the symbols and pictures of spiritual realities. They belong to this present sphere of sensuous and transient existence and do not rise to the sphere of eternal, spiritual realities. Yet that the law is so characterized must never be supposed to militate against its divine origin and character. It is of divine origin, but it is at the same time imperfect and provisional. Its highest dignity and honor are found in the fact that it ministers to the bringing in of the Gospel. As Luther justly insists, we are to remember that Paul's seeming depreciation of the law, is in view of its utter inability to justify. Luther however speaks too strongly when he says: "Because Paul is here in the matter of justification, it was necessary that he should speak of the law as a thing very contemptible and odious."

4. But when the fulness of the time came, God sent forth his Son, born of a woman, born under the law:—The fulness here denotes, "that which fills up something," *complementum;* the meaning is, when the time which completes the period of waiting, came. The coming of Christ into the world is at the end of a destined time of preparation during which the consciousness of a need of salvation should be developed, as is evident from iii. 19, 24, and from Rom. v. 20, 21.

The words: **God sent forth his Son,** certainly presuppose the preëxistence of Christ, as do the kindred expressions in Rom. viii. 3; II Cor. vii. 9, and especially the *locus classicus*, Phil. ii. 5 *seq*. In Col. i. 15, Christ is called "the image of the invisible God, the first-born of every creature," that is, the embodiment and revelation of the Father and the one whose existence antedates that of every created thing, and is also described (v. 16) as the one through whom is mediated the creation of all things. That Paul teaches the personal preëxistence of Christ is not denied by competent scholars whether they themselves hold that doctrine or not.

It is commonly thought that the logical starting-point for the development of the doctrine of the preëxistence with Paul is his view of the exalted Christ. Perhaps, in that case, the idea of the incarnation and humiliation, as found especially in II Cor. viii. 9 and Phil. ii. 5, *seq.*, would come next in logical order of development. But these three ideas certainly belong inseparably together in the Pauline system, and no chronological order in their development can be confidently determined.

Born of a woman (γενόμενον ἐκ γυναικός),—to show that he came in a human manner into human life, while the words, **born under the law** (γεν. ὑπὸ νόμον), emphasize the idea of his coming into full natural relations as a Jew. He was a real man and a real Jew. The participle as employed the second time should have the same sense as in the first case, viz.: **born.** (So R. V. vs. A. V.). The phrase **born of a woman** does not intimate any idea of a supernatural birth, nor does Paul elsewhere. He may have known nothing of this subject, which lay outside the current apostolic tradition, and may not have gained currency in the church until considerably later, as a result of subsequent inquiries, (*cf.* Luke i. 1–4). Paul has nowhere given any intimation on this subject. It is too much to say (with Pfleiderer) that he denies the supernatural generation of Christ. He says that Christ is "according to the flesh" (κατὰ σάρκα), son of David

(Rom. i. 3), which would be just as true in literal fact, if he was the putative son of Joseph, provided the genealogy of Luke is that of Mary, since that genealogy traces Christ's descent through David's line. It is evident that the Apostle regards it as a necessary condition of saving men that the Christ should come into their condition. He is born **under the law** that "he might redeem them which were under the law," (v. 5). The thought is similar in Rom. viii. 3; Christ entered into the sphere of the flesh that he might destroy the power of sin which rules there. What is the causal connection between Christ's taking the condition of those whom he would save and the salvation itself? Or, to put the question more specifically, and with reference to our present passage, why, according to Paul, must Christ become subject to the law in order to save those who are under it, (the Jews)?

The following views may be noted:

(1) It was that, by perfect obedience to the law, he might exhibit the true life and thus set men upon the course of a similar life of obedience.

(2) It was that this perfect obedience might be imputed to the disobedient. He came under the law and perfectly obeyed it, and his obedience serves for ours by being reckoned to us.

The following difficulties have been urged against this view:

(a) The point in the discussion turns upon saving the Jews (οἱ ὑπὸ νόμον), and not upon the doctrine of salvation in general. The view overlooks the Pauline use of law (= the Mosaic law), and makes it signify moral law in general. *Per contra*, it is said, that law is for Paul the concrete embodiment of divine or moral law in general. But is Paul so treating it here in our passage? It can hardly be maintained that he is.

(*b*) There is no mention in Paul's writings of the imputation of Christ's obedience to us. Two things are said to be imputed: faith (generally), and righteousness (not Christ's personal righteousness, but that *status* or character of righteousness into which faith introduces us), so that these two resolve into precisely the same thing.

(3) It may be held that Gal. iii. 13 furnishes the key for the solution of the question. Christ redeems the Jews from the curse by coming under the law and receiving its curse upon himself. Bearing the curse for them he can liberate them from it. There still remains the difficulty mentioned above [denoted by (*a*)] which, however, may be solved on Pauline principles by the view presented in Rom. i. that the Gentiles are also under law in the sense of having a revelation of God in nature and in conscience which renders them without excuse and proves them sinful and guilty. If so, then the " curse " which rested upon the Gentiles, came upon Christ as truly as that which rested upon the

Jews, and in the same sense. This view, if taken, decides nothing as to the exact sense in which Christ assumed the curse,—a question to which Paul has given no explicit answer. He, however, points out (Rom. iii. 25), that it was in such a way as to reveal God's righteousness and to show him to be just in effecting this work of Christ, while he, at the same time, graciously provides salvation for sinful men. Doubtless Christ comes under the law, first of all, that he may perfectly obey the law: Rom. v. 19, "on account of the obedience of one many are made righteous;" II Cor. v. 21, "He made him to be sin for us who knew no sin, that we might become the righteousness of God in him." How should his obedience accomplish this result for and in us? Perhaps because, though obeying the law perfectly, he yet comes under its curse (becomes a "curse,"—becomes "sin"), thus showing that this curse does not come upon him on his own account, but is assumed vicariously for us. His perfect obedience is thus the condition precedent of his vicarious suffering, because if he had not been perfectly obedient, he would have deserved the curse and must have borne it for himself and not for us. His perfect obedience avails for us, according to Paul, neither, primarily, by way of example, nor by way of imputation, but by being the essential prerequisite of the vicarious bearing of the curse on our behalf. Neither does this fact determine the sense in which he bears the curse, —which always remains a problem of speculative theology,—but only gives the form and order of the Pauline thought.

5. That he might redeem them which were under the law, that we might receive the adoption of sons.—In the second clause: **that we might receive,** etc., the thought which had been moving in the Jewish sphere, broadens to embrace all Christians, whether Jewish or Gentile, as the recipients of the adoption. The word rendered **receive** (lit. to "receive back," ἀπολάβωμεν), is understood: (a) to receive back what was lost in Adam, (so Augustine). A fatal objection to this view is, that it makes υἱοθεσία mean "sonship," whereas it means **adoption;** (b) to receive back as due or destined for us, as the result of the promise; (c) to receive from (ἀπό), the redemption, as its fruit or consequence; (d) simply **receive** (= λάβωμεν) (so, Meyer, R. V.) Usage favors making ἀπολ. express something more than λάβωμεν and very probably the idea of either (b) or (c) may be implied, though it is, perhaps, impracticable to recognize it in translation.

6. And because ye are sons, God sent forth the Spirit of his Son into our hearts, crying, Abba, Father.—The "adoption" being now accomplished in objective fact, the Apostle next alludes to the subjective certitude of it. Because ye (without distinction of Jew and Gentile) are sons, did God send forth his Spirit, which could not have been done for those under the bondage of the law. The possession of the Spirit is at once the consequence and the proof of sonship. The specific designation, **the Spirit of his Son,** is no doubt chosen with regard to the term **sons** above. Since ye are sons, God has sent the Spirit of him who is preëminently God's Son. Ye share the same Spirit with the divine Son. The term means distinctively the Holy Spirit. The believer is conceived of as being the organ of the Holy Spirit, who, entering his heart, cries aloud, $i.\ e.$, enables the man to say, **Abba, Father,** by inspiring within him the consciousness and experience of sonship to God. $Cf.$ Rom. viii. 15. The point is that the Holy Spirit inspires the sense of sonship.

Abba, Father ('Αββᾶ ὁ πατήρ), is a somewhat stereotyped phrase (Rom. viii. 15; Mark xiv. 36), evidently resulting from the use of the Aramaic word "Abba" in prayer; but whether from Christ's own use of it (as Meyer supposes), or only from its use by the Jews cannot be determined. Others suppose that "Father" is added only to explain the word "Abba" to Gentile readers, but it probably was too common to need such explanation. $Cf.$ the devotional use in many languages of the Hebrew "Amen."

7. So that thou art no longer a bondservant, but a son; and if a son, then an heir through God.—This is the application to the individual (**thou art**), of the conclusion that Christians are sons and heirs. It is here seen that Paul treats the **bondage** (δουλεία) as practically belonging to the Gentiles as well as the Jews under the law, showing that, in principle, the bondage and curse of the Jews under the law was representative of the state of the whole world. Thou (Jew or Gentile) art not a **bondservant,** (δοῦλος) (which therefore each had been), but a son, and if a son also an heir. The inheritance here spoken of refers to the Messianic blessedness which God had promised. Now only the *sons* inherit, hence sonship and inheritance are one and indivisible. We may here note the transitions of thought, from Jews in 5 (*a*), to all Christians in 5 (*b*); and from Christians in general in 6 (*a*), to the individual Christian in 6 (*b*). For the expression **through God** (διὰ θεοῦ), the *Textus Receptus* (so A. V.) reads "of God through Christ" (θεοῦ διὰ Χριστοῦ). The former reading is overwhelmingly attested and is adopted by all recent critics. The sense probably is: an heir through the adopting act of God. The representation throughout this passage is prevailingly that of sonship by adoption, and not, as with John, that of sonship to God by new birth. If the former figure is kept in mind, the appar-

The Epistle to the Galatians.

ent harshness of the reading "through God" is lessened. It may have been the overlooking of this fact by copyists which occasioned the gloss found in the *Textus Receptus*.

II. THE STAGE OF RELIGIOUS DEVELOPMENT REPRESENTED BY THE LAW, 8–11.

8. Howbeit at that time, not knowing God, ye were in bondage to them which by nature are no gods.—Paul here alludes to their ignorant condition as unconverted heathen in contrast to their ideal Christian position. **Howbeit** (ἀλλά) points this contrast between their true and proper sonship to God, previously described, and the fact that they now desire to return to a condition as far below it as that in which they were at their conversion. The terms, **at that time** (τότε μέν) and "but now" (νῦν δέ, ver. 9), contrast their past ignorance with their present knowledge, notwithstanding which they are ready to fall down upon the lower plane of **bondage.** As once in service to those beings which are not in their real nature gods, but only "so-called gods" (λεγόμενοι θεοί), (see I Cor. viii. 5), and in reality "demons" (δαιμόνια) (see I Cor. x. 20), it might be thought that they would appreciate and use their better knowledge. Thus Paul puts the present Jewish-Christian and the present Heathen-Christian state in the same category. The one he describes as a "childhood," to the other he imputes "ignorance;" both are a "bondage," both religions are elementary,—illustrations of the "rudiments of the world."

9. But now that ye have come to know God, or rather to be known of God, how turn ye back again to the weak and beggarly rudiments, whereunto ye desire to be in bondage over again?—**Now that ye have come to know God** (γνόντες θεόν): This verb denotes "to know by ascertaining," while the word used in the previous verse (εἰδότες) refers rather to the possession of knowledge: "Not yourselves possessing the knowledge of God (εἰδότες), but after having learned of him (γνόντες). **Or rather** (μᾶλλον δέ) is a quasi-correction, for greater clearness and fulness, adding also a statement of the divine side of the matter, perhaps, as Meyer suggests, in order to make their threatened lapse appear more clearly as a desertion of God, thus: "You are not only forsaking what you know, but him who has known you, taught you, loved you." The statement of this knowledge on its divine side, as an outgoing of divine interest in them, adds a further element of culpability to their retrograde movement. **How turn ye back again** (πῶς ἐπιστρέφετε πάλιν) expresses the Apostle's surprise and indignation. **Again** having been, for the most part, heathen (and not Jews) before their conversion, their religion was rudimentary, so "*again*" is it to be, if under the influence of the Judaizers, they go back from Christianity to Mosaism. The Apostle assures them that the worship and service to which they are going is as truly an example of "the weak and beggarly rudiments of the world" (τὰ ἀσθενῆ καὶ πτωχὰ στοιχεῖα) as that from which they came. This is Paul's most depreciatory characterization of the Mosaic system and yet it is "weak" not as being a mere human system, but as being powerless to justify (*cf.* iii. 21; Rom. viii. 3,—τὸ ἀδύνατον τοῦ νόμου); it is "poor" as being unable to confer that rich benefit of sonship and peace which is the gift of God through faith in Christ. How completely Paul puts the heathen and Jewish religions upon the same plane is here clearly seen in the force of "again," and in both being called **rudiments** (the former by implication, the latter directly); but it is to be carefully noted that it is in respect to their powerlessness to justify that he puts them into the same category. Paul's view of the Old Testament system, as elsewhere expounded, would render his putting them upon the same plane in origin and character, utterly impossible.

Over again (πάλιν ἀνωθεν); The latter of these words may have either of three meanings: (1) "from above," its strict, original signification; (2) "from the beginning," and so, (3) "over again." To me (3) seems improbable because we have the word "again" (πάλιν), which suffices for that idea;

(1) gives, in this passage, no proper sense. I therefore prefer (2) so that the two terms together express emphatically the idea of going back to the "rudiments" *again* and commencing religious development *from the beginning*. The only passage where much doubt or importance attaches to the meaning of this word (ἄνωθεν) is John iii. 3 "born *again*" (A. V.),—"*anew*" (R. V.),—"from above" (R. V. marg.). It is here most commonly explained as meaning "from above," but the wonder of Nicodemus was in regard to being born a *second time* from which it is a natural inference that he understood the word in the question of Jesus to mean "again." The old interpretation is, in my judgment, to be preferred.

10. Ye observe days, and months, and seasons, and years.—Many punctuate this sentence interrogatively (as Tischendorf, Meyer, Alford, Lightfoot); others with a period (Westcott and Hort, Ellicott). In the former case, verse 10 continues the surprised and indignant questioning of verse 9. In the latter, it introduces positive proof of their desire to be enslaved again. Either yields a good sense. This observance of days, etc., was clearly a Jewish observance. **Days** would naturally refer to Jewish feast or fast days, and sabbaths, in respect to which (according to Col. ii. 16) no one is to judge the Christian, and which are a shadow of things to come. **Months** are commonly supposed to refer to the new moons (also mentioned in Col. ii. 16).

Others suppose that some particular months of the year are meant. The seventh (Tisri) as the sabbatic month had a sacred character, (Meyer). **Seasons** (καιρούς) would naturally embrace such festal occasions, as Passover, Pentecost and the Feast of Booths; while **years** (ἐνιαυτούς), would doubtless refer to the sabbatic years, and perhaps to the year of Jubilee (which, however, some maintain had long before fallen into abeyance). He charges them with taking up the observance of this system of sacred times and seasons, not because it is evil in itself, but because it marks on their part a retrograde movement in religion. In regard to these observances, so far as their merits were concerned, the Apostle's position was conciliatory and his spirit that of concession (Rom. xiv. 5-6; Col. ii. 16); but, in the present situation, a principle was at stake and must not be compromised. He is opposed to all participation in these Jewish observances because they are regarded as necessary to salvation; they thus threaten the sole sufficiency of faith. Compare his attitude toward circumcision in general, (Acts xvi. 3; Gal. vi. 15; I Cor. ix. 20); but, note how strenuously he is opposed to it when it is sought to be forced upon one (Titus) who would have no reason to choose it for himself, and where the claim savored of enforcing it as a necessity to salvation. The explanation of Lightfoot, who supposes a division of the law into spiritual and ritualistic elements, is not in accord with the *unity* of the law.

11. I am afraid of you, lest by any means I have bestowed labor upon you in vain:—You after **I am afraid of** (φοβοῦμαι) probably designates them as the objects of his anxious solicitude. "I am afraid in regard to you" (so Meyer, Ellicott). By many the accusative (ὑμᾶς) is explained as a case of attraction or assimilation to the case of the **you** in the following subordinate clause (so Winer, Wieseler). The indicative after **lest** (μήπως) denotes his apprehension that it is really the fact that he has bestowed his labor in vain *i. e.* without bringing them to permanent Christian life and character.

III. EXHORTATION TO THE GALATIANS TO RETURN TO THE TRUE CHRISTIAN POSITION, 12–20.

12. I beseech you, brethren, be as I am, for I am as ye are.—After the censure of the previous verses, the Apostle adopts a more persuasive tone; his language changes from that of discouragement to that of entreaty and hopefulness in regard to their defections from the faith. "Become as I am, because I became (*sc.* ἐγενόμην) as you." Because I, who was a Jew by nature and conviction, became as a Gentile for your sakes, you should now reciprocate by renouncing your Judaism and coming to my standing-point. I became as a Gentile in order that I might bring you to a state where there is neither Jew nor Greek, but where all stand above these distinctions in Christ. The "becoming" on Paul's part is fully described in I Cor. ix. 20-23. When he says "Become as I" he is referring to the true Christian position as contrasted with narrow and prejudiced national Christianity. What he says in no way involves the setting forth of himself as a model of perfection. His thought is: "I make this conciliatory and persuasive appeal on the ground of our friendly relations; when I was among you you did me no injustice; I may therefore hopefully appeal to you now to grant my reasonable and just request.

13. Ye did me no wrong: but ye know that because of an infirmity of the flesh I preached the gospel unto you the first time.—"So far from doing me injustice," continues the Apostle, "you sympathized with me in my infirmity and patiently bore the trial which my infirmity caused. Nay, you received me with the greatest honor and reverence." These conciliatory and persuasive expressions were adapted to secure a favorable consideration of his exhortation. The word **but** (δέ) forms the transition to that description of their kindness which is contrasted with the idea of doing him injustice (ἠδικήσατε). The force of verse 13 depends upon the meaning of the word rendered, "because of" (διά); usage strongly favors this meaning, *i. e.* by reason of an illness I was detained among you when I came and preached to you, and from this illness arose a trial for you, a care and embarrassment, which, however, you kindly bore, even treating me with excessive consideration. (So Meyer, Ellicott, and Lightfoot). Others, (as Olshausen, Ewald) explain this preposition as meaning "in the experience of" (= ἐν), which gives substantially the same sense, though not assigning his weakness as the cause of his remaining and preaching. Others, (as De Wette, Wieseler), explain the reference in the **infirmity of the flesh,** not to Paul, but to the Galatians, and translate: "on account of the weakness of your flesh," a view of the passage which does not naturally explain the reference in the next verse to the trial ("temptation"— πειρασμός), which Paul occasioned the Galatians and their patience in bearing it.

The first time, *i. e.* at his first visit, when he established Christianity in Galatia (Acts xvi. 6). The second visit is mentioned in Acts xviii. 23.

14. And that which was a temptation to you in my flesh ye despised not, nor rejected; but ye received me as an angel of God, even as Christ Jesus.—The older texts read, "My temptation" (πειρασμόν μου): *cf.* A. V. According to this reading the meaning is, my trial (the trial which God sent upon me) you did not despise nor disdainfully reject; *i. e.* you were not indifferent to my feeble condition and did not reject me in consequence of it. But the reading, "your temptation" (πειρασμὸν ὑμῶν) is much better supported (A B D F G ℵ Copt. Vulg. It.), according to which the meaning is: But your proof or trial (viz. that which was occasioned by my infirmity), you did not reject, or refuse to submit to. On the contrary you bore the test which my condition imposed. What this sickness was we do not know. The terms **despised** and **rejected** (ἐξουθενήσατε οὐδὲ ἐξεπτύσατε) are strong words hardly appropriate to the object, **temptation**, especially the latter verb; but they express in a hyperbolic way the idea of rejection in order to point the contrast with their actual reception of him as an angel, and even as Christ himself—in whose name he had come,—equally emphatic statements of their conduct, and together reflecting the enthusiastic but mercurial character of the Galatians.

15. Where then is that gratulation of yourselves? for I bear you witness, that, if possible, ye would have plucked out your eyes and given them to me.—The meaning of the question, **Where then** etc., probably is: Where then is your felicitation of yourselves; your self-congratulation and joy in my labors? It is nowhere. What a change has come over you! How different now your attitude and feeling toward me! The word **for** (γάρ) refers to the **gratulation** mentioned. It was a great self-gratulation *for* you were so devoted that you would have given me your very eyes. Many suppose that the allusion implies that Paul had some malady of the eyes, a defect which the Galatians would, if possible, have been willing to supply, but he is probably merely using a popular hyperbole.

16. So then am I become your enemy, because I tell you the truth?—He here abruptly introduces a question which presents the consequence (ὥστε) of that cooling of their ardor which is alluded to in ver. 15. Your joy and satisfaction in my labors are no more. Your devotion is gone. Has it accordingly come to this, that I have become your enemy because I spoke the truth to you? **Your enemy** (ἐχθρὸς ὑμῶν) is probably active in force; "hostile to you," though, of course, mutual hostility is involved. The time when he thinks of himself as having become their enemy is not that at which the Epistle was read (so Jerome, Luther), for that was yet future; nor that of the first visit (for then he experienced only the regard spoken of above), but that of the second visit, when the seeds of Judaism had, no doubt, already been sown, and the germs of the future troubles planted. The solemn affirmations of i. 9 and v. 3 probably refer to reproofs of the Galatians by Paul while with them, during the second visit.

17. They zealously seek you in no good way; nay, they desire to shut you out, that ye may seek them.—The mention of a feeling of hostility between themselves and him, calls to his mind the persons to whom he had become hostile, that is, the Jewish extremists, and the affirmation of verse 17 refers to them. They are zealous for you; *i. e.* they interest themselves to draw you over to their side; **in no good way** (οὐ καλῶς) *i. e.* in a party spirit, not in a way to promote your true good. Their proselytism proceeds from narrow conceptions of Christianity and cannot issue in a real benefit to you. **Nay, they desire to shut you out** (ἐκκλεῖσαι ὑμᾶς θέλουσιν), **that ye may seek them**, *i. e.* in order that you may zealously seek (pay court to, ἵνα αὐτοὺς ζηλοῦτε) them. Shut you out from what? Many answers have been given: (*a*) From Paul and from communion with him (Winer, Bengel, Olshausen); (*b*) from the whole body of Christians (Flatt); (*c*) from all Christians thinking differently (Schott); (*d*) from true knowledge (Chrysostom, Theophylact); (*e*) from Christian freedom (Erasmus); (*f*) from Christ and confidence in him (Luther); (*g*) from the kingdom of truth (Matthies); (*h*) from the kingdom of heaven (Wieseler); (*i*) from salvation by faith (Matthias); (*j*) from other teachers, who do not be-

The True Christian Position: iv. 18. 179

long to their way of thinking, (Meyer, Ellicott). This is the preferable view as shown by the following clause, which states the aim of this "shutting out." The purpose of the Judaizing sectaries is, that they may cut the Galatians off from that larger Christian fellowship which Paul advocates and represents, and thus oblige them to cling zealously to themselves (the Judaizers). "They wish to make you exclusive," says the Apostle, "so as to attach you to themselves." It should be noticed that the telic conjunction **that** (ἵνα), is here used with the indicative, as in I Cor. iv. 6, an unclassical construction, (so explained by most critics, including Lightfoot, Ellicott, Winer, Olshausen, Wieseler). Meyer, however, contends that ἵνα here is local, meaning "where," and referring to the Jewish Christian sphere.

18. But it is good to be zealously sought in a good matter at all times, and not only when I am present with you.—The Apostle now assures his readers that he does not object to their being **zealously sought** in itself. But the instance in question is a case of perverted zeal. "It is good to be zealously sought, to have one's favor courted in a good way or cause, but they are not courting it in this way. It is well that this zeal should be always operative in this good way and not merely when I am with you." The words **at all times, and not only when,**

etc., seem to mean: "I could wish you to be always the object of zealous attention from others; I cannot always be with you to direct your religious life, but I greatly desire that this zeal of others for you be sincere and be directed not by party-spirit but by an interest in your spiritual growth."

19. My little children, of whom I am again in travail until Christ be formed in you.—Paul now ends his rebuke in a strain of tenderness, and with a singularly complex metaphor, in which he not only represents himself as the mother bringing forth the child **(I am again in travail,** etc.), but instead of carrying out that violent figure, adds to its confusion by speaking, not of their being born, but of Christ as being formed within them. Practically what he means is, that it seems as if he must convert them over again to Christ, so sadly have they fallen away.

20. Yea, I could wish to be present with you now, and to change my voice; for I am perplexed about you.—But (**yea,** δὲ)—speaking of being present with you (v. 18),—I could wish (if such a thing were possible), to be present with you. **I could wish** (ἤθελον) is the apodosis (without the classical ἄν) corresponding to an implied protasis, and denoting a conclusion whose fulfillment is out of the question, *cf.* Rom. ix. 3. **To change my voice** means, to adopt a more winsome manner of dealing with your apostasy which the Apostle thinks, if he were among them, might prove effectual. He could wish this because he is in perplexity about them as to whether he has dealt with them in the wisest and most effectual way, and he would gladly make every possible effort.

IV. A NARRATIVE FROM THE LAW ITSELF MAY BE ALLEGORICALLY APPLIED SO AS TO ILLUSTRATE THE TRUTH THAT THOSE WHO ADHERE TO THE LAW ARE IN BONDAGE, 21–v. 1.

These verses should first be observed in their connection. The passage is an *argumentum ad hominem*. In its form it would be harmonious with modes of handling the Old Testament familiar and valid with those to whom it is addressed.

21. Tell me, ye that desire to be under the law, do ye not hear the law? He here appeals to the devotees of the law to take a lesson out of the law.

22. For it is written, that Abraham had two sons, one by the handmaid, and one by the freewoman. This verse states the case: Abraham had two sons, who, from the circumstances of their birth, may be contemplated as representing two principles, *bondage* and *freedom*.

23. Howbeit the son by the handmaid is born after the flesh; but the son by the freewoman is born through promise.—He next states the *ground* of this application of the matter. The one, as being the son of a bondwoman, is a child **after the flesh** (κατὰ σάρκα), and represents the earthly and carnal; while the other child, being born in fulfillment of a divine promise (δι ἐπαγγελίας), stands in relation to that which is higher and spiritual.

24. Which things contain an allegory: for these women are two covenants; one from mount Sinai, bearing children unto bondage, which is Hagar.—The allegorical application is now made: The character of these two, as connected with their birth, fitly represents the respective principles of the two covenants, the old and the new; descent in Hagar's line symbolizes the bondage and the carnal element in the Old Testament system, while descent from Sarah expresses promise, freedom, and typifies spiritual life. The former stands for the Sinai covenant.

25. Now this Hagar is mount Sinai in Arabia, and answereth to the Jerusalem that now is: for she is in bondage with her children.—In this verse a local consideration is thrown in which makes his allegory the more appropriate: * " I may fitly represent the Sinai-covenant

---

* This explanation proceeds upon my preference for the text which is followed by the marginal translation of the R. V., and which is discussed a little further on. *Cf.* the paraphrase and the fuller note on ver. 25, p. 187, *seq*.

by Hagar, because Sinai is situated in Arabia, the land of Hagar's descendants. Or, to liken it to something else which stands for the old covenant as truly as Sinai does, it corresponds to the Jerusalem of Judaism, the earthly and temporal city, which is the center of the old dispensation, whose children (the Jews still under the law) are in a state of bondage. But there is *another* Jerusalem, a heavenly city, the city of God, the spiritual commonwealth whose law is freedom, that is, Christianity, to which the promise looked forward. In this city the joyous promises to the desolate are realized, and here we find the inheritance to which the ancient gracious covenant with Abraham respecting Isaac looked forward (27-30). Apart from the allegorical form, what is the real thought of the passage? Simply this: The characteristic quality and effect of the two covenants, externality and bondage on the one hand, spirituality and freedom on the other, are represented and illustrated by the natural relations of bondage and freedom in the case of the two women, Hagar and Sarah, and in the case of their descendants. Apart from the allegorical form of the argument (which is very sparingly used by Paul), we have here simply the use of the differing relations of these two women to Abraham, and the historic relations of the two lines of descent, to illustrate the respective principles of the two covenants. The form of thought is Rabbinic as in the case of the argument upon the words "seed" and "seeds" (iii. 16), and in the application of the passage "Thou shalt not muzzle the ox," etc. (I Cor. ix. 9) to Christian teachers; but, apart from this, the parallel instituted is ingenious and appropriate, and this fact is all that is essential in the case. Two points should be remembered: (1) How sparingly and temperately Paul uses the allegorical method, a remarkable fact when his strict Pharisaic training is considered; and (2) that there is no case, in which he uses the allegorical form of argument, where, if the form were dropped, a forcible and valid argument could not still be derived and developed from the relations which the allegory contemplates. It was a keen and true observation of Luther that Paul's allegorical arguments were the painting of the house *after it had been built*.

These verses may now be considered more in detail. (21) **Do ye not hear the law** (τὸν νόμον οὐκ ἀκούετε;), is generally understood to mean: "Will you not listen to the law, attend to a lesson out of your venerated law?" The present tense rather favors the interpretation: "Do you not hear the law read in your synagogue service?" (So Usteri, Meyer, Ellicott). The appeal is to those who are inclined to hold the view that the Mosaic law is binding on Christians. Ver. 22 refers to no single passage, but to the history recorded in Genesis Chs. xvi. and xxi.

23. The emphasis is laid upon the two sets of contrasted terms **handmaid** and **free woman, after the flesh,** and **through promise**; the first pair of terms setting forth the principles of bondage and freedom which the Apostle is to apply to the two covenants; and the second pair expressing, on the one hand, the carnal, outward and temporary relations of Hagar and her son Ishmael and his descendants, as connected with Abraham, and on the other hand, the spiritual and permanent relations symbolized in the birth of Isaac according to a divine promise,—relations which are paralleled in the spiritual system of Christianity, which is the ideal fulfillment of these ancient promises and covenants. The word "through" (διά), ascribes the birth of Isaac to the agency of the promise, in the sense that it was due to that divine operation which lay behind tho promise as the guaranty of its fulfillment.

24. Which things (= *quippe quae*) **contain an allegory** (or, are spoken allegorically).

Two general views are commonly taken of this assertion:—

I. Paul meant that the facts under consideration could be *treated* allegorically, though not necessarily affirming that they contained an allegory in the purpose of the writer. On this view, the allegory is found only in Paul's own use and application of the history (so Lightfoot).

II. He meant that this history contained an allegorical meaning in addition to the historical; that the facts narrated concerning the persons here referred to, contained, in the thought of the writer, or, in the purpose of divine providence, a hidden, spiritual sense which referred to the nature and relations of the two covenants (so Chrysostom, Weiss, Ellicott).

There is, in any case, no good reason to suppose that the Apostle here set aside the historical sense and replaced it by the allegorical meaning; (*cf.*, however, I Cor. ix. 9, 10, where if πάντως mean "altogether" (R. V.) and not "certainly," the historical sense seems to be set aside). The second explanation is more probably correct in that form of it which holds, not that it was the conscious purpose of the writer to compose an allegory when writing the Genesis narratives (as the A. V. might imply by rendering: "which things are an allegory"); but that there was, in the divine thought, a typical and mystical meaning in this history which was revealed and fulfilled in the gospel.

This interpretation seems probable on two grounds: (*a*) It is natural to expect that Paul would not be wholly free from the Rabbinic habits of thought in which he had been trained, prominent among which was the allegorical method of interpretation which sought a hidden sense, a spiritual meaning, in the historical narratives of the Old

An Allegorical Illustration from the Law: iv. 25.

Testament, not merely as being suggested or typified by them, but as being contained in them and as intended by the writers, or, at any rate, by the divine mind. (*b*) Paul's actual use, in a few other clear instances, (I Cor. ix. 9, 10; Gal. iii. 16 and II Cor. iii. 13, 14) of allegorical interpretations, where it can hardly be doubted that he finds the figurative meaning in the passages, and does not merely develop it from them by way of application or illustration, renders the supposition that he does so in this case also extremely probable.

25. The word **Hagar** (Ἁγαρ) is omitted by ℵ C F G Aeth., Armen., Vulg., Goth. and by the Latin Fathers; deleted by Tischendorf, Lightfoot, Lachmann, margin of R. V., Wieseler; and bracketed by Westcott and Hort. It is sustained by A. B D K L P, the Cursive Mss., Chrysostom, Meyer, T. R., A. V., R. V. If retained, the meaning is: "The name Hagar is applied to Mount Sinai, and this fact establishes the connection between the bondwoman Hagar and Mount Sinai as the symbol of the Old Testament." If it is omitted, the sense would be: "Mount Sinai is in Arabia, the land of Hagar's descendants." The allegorizing element is larger in the former reading and the connection more artificial. Apart from the external evidence, it appears to me that the slight modification of the text so as to suggest an allegorical connection of thought by affirming the iden-

tity of the names Hagar and Sinai can be more easily supposed, than can the omission of this word, if originally written; also, that it is unlikely that Paul would think of, or even know, such a fact as that in Arabia Mount Sinai was called by a name closely resembling "Hagar." This view introduces an element which is generally felt to be more artificial and extraneous. The search for a name sounding like Hagar as an appellation for Mount Sinai has not been clearly successful. (See Meyer *in loco*, and Lightfoot's Excursus on the point). The evidence is indeed closely balanced, but I believe that, on the whole, the probability is against the reading of Ἁγαρ here.

And now, after establishing a connection between Arabia, the land of the bondwoman's descendants, and Sinai, the same purpose is further subserved by joining Sinai and Jerusalem. Sinai corresponds to Jerusalem; both alike are symbols of the old covenant. The allegorical correlative of Hagar and her country is Sinai, but since Sinai and Jerusalem signify the same, Jerusalem may, with equal propriety, take the place of Sinai. If "Hagar" is read in ver. 25, then that name (note the neuter τὸ Ἁγαρ, as denoting the *name* and not the *person* Hagar) is the subject of the verb "answereth" (συνστοιχεῖ); but if not, then the subject is "Sinai" considered as the symbol of the Old Testament system. But "Jerusalem," regarded in this same relation, is probably the subject of "is in bondage" (δουλεύει) in either case. At this point the figure of Jerusalem as a mother of children creeps in, so that Jerusalem can be said to be in bondage with her children. The figure becomes explicit in verse 26. The simple sense here is that the Old Testament system is a system of bondage, as opposed to the freedom of the gospel, because the law lays upon men burdens of obligation which by reason of sin and weakness they cannot lift, and then the law shuts them up in ward until the grace of God, which is the principle of the gospel, sets them free. The bondage is the result of the guilt which the law can charge upon man, but from which it cannot deliver him.

26. But the Jerusalem that is above is free, which is our mother.—The contrast to the Old Testament system in this respect, to this present earthly Jerusalem, (ἡ νῦν Ἱερουσαλήμ) is the upper Jerusalem, the spiritual Jerusalem, (ἡ ἄνω Ἱερ.) the city and commonwealth of God whose principle is freedom and which is the mother of whom we believers, the children of promise, are born. Note then, the two correlative sets of terms and ideas. They are, on the one side: Hagar, a bondwoman; Ishmael, a son born in mere carnal relations; his descendants inhabiting a land of bondage. To this series of facts, correspond the character and effects of the Old Testament system, which shuts sinners up in bondage. On the other side: Sarah, who bears a child of promise, and who, with her descendants, illustrates the principles of the kingdom of God which sets men free from their sins; to which kingdom we belong. The analogy is not only ingenious, but striking and appropriate.

27. For it is written Rejoice, thou barren that bearest not;

Break forth and cry, thou that travailest not:

For more are the children of the desolate than of her which hath the husband.
—The figure of the mother (Jerusalem) who had been prefigured by Sarah, once childless, but later the glad mother of a child of promise, suggests an Old Testament passage where the same figure had been applied to Jerusalem the holy city in its desolation during the exile (Isa. liv. 1). In the exile, the forsaken city is congratulated in hope of the return of her people and of renewed prosperity. This language is now applied to the spiritual Jerusalem whose children (the faithful) shall be numerous, though descended from the long childless Sarah. The passage is at least indirectly Messianic in the Old Testament, inasmuch as the theocratic Jerusalem is a type of the "upper Jerusalem." The application of the figure is not to be forced beyond this limit. The woman that "hath the husband" is the theocracy; the "barren" one is the Christian church, but these terms are applied in keeping

with the Old Testament sense of the passage and are not to be forced rigidly through in the application.

28. Now we, brethren, as Isaac was, are children of promise.—This verse contains the application of the allegory to the Apostle's practical purpose. He declares: "You Christians belong to this free lineage which stands in the line of promise connected with Isaac." Here it is seen how the whole force of his "allegory" bears upon the Judaizers. "When you go over to the law again and cling to it, it is as if you were determined to prove yourselves Hagar's descendants, and so to give up your true lineage and privileges. **As Isaac** (κατὰ 'Ισαάκ), refers to the promise connected with his birth, a promise which extends itself to, and is fulfilled in, all believers. Faith is that which assures to us the inheritance of the promises.

29. But as then he that was born after the flesh persecuted him that was born after the Spirit, even so it is now.—The "persecution" of Isaac by Ishmael is explained in two ways: (1) The reference is to Gen. xxi. 9, where on the feast day when Isaac was weaned, it is said that Sarah saw Ishmael "mocking" (R. V. text) or "laughing" (margin). The Hebrew verb meaning to laugh (צָחַק), does sometimes mean "to laugh contemptuously;" *i. e.* to mock, and is generally so understood in that passage. This interpretation would harmonize with the sequel where Hagar and her son are sent away for this act of Ishmael. But this "mocking" does not amount to "persecution." Another explanation, somewhat different, but still resting on Gen. xxi. 9, is sometimes given: This act of mocking is typical of the hostile relations of the descendants of Hagar to Israel (Ps. lxxxiii. 7; I Chron. v. 10, 19). It is very probable that Paul contemplates the personal relations of the two sons as typical of the relations of their descendants, but it still remains the sons personally to which this language applies. The LXX. understood the original word here (מְצַחֵק) to mean "laughing," "playing," and rendered "playing with Isaac her son" (παίζοντα κ. τ. λ.). (2) The reference is to the Jewish tradition which was developed on the basis of Gen. xxi. 9, according to which Isaac was tormented by his half-brother. Meyer quotes an example of this tradition: "Ishmael said to Isaac, Let us go and see our portion in the field; and Ishmael carried the bow and arrows, and shot at Isaac, and acted as though he were in sport." This is doubtless what formed the basis of Paul's statement, but, as stated above, these relations are contemplated as representative. **So it is now,** that is, so now the Jews (Christians who will still be Jews, Judaizers), who still cling to the bondage system, persecute the adherents of Christianity. Others (as Meyer) refer this persecution to the hard-

An Allegorical Illustration from the Law: iv. 30. 193

ships which the Christians suffered from the literal Jews. In principle, both would be included.

30. Howbeit what saith the scripture? Cast out the handmaid and her son: for the son of the handmaid shall not inherit with the son of the freewoman.—The result of these hostile relations is now depicted. As the mocking son of the bondwoman was cast out of the family to wander forsaken, so shall the Jewish opposition to the spiritual kingdom of God be terminated by God's providential judgment. The Scripture cited is the language of Sarah, (Gen. xxi. 10), confirmed by the command of God in verse 12.

31. Wherefore, brethren, we are not children of a handmaid, but of the freewoman.—This is the practical conclusion and application of the whole allegory. As the bondwoman was cast out, so is the Jewish system, which she typified, set aside. We belong to a different and higher lineage and order. This statement clearly involves the obligation to be devoted to the Christian system and not longer to confuse it with that of the law from which the readers, as Christians, are free.

ANALYSIS AND PARAPHRASE OF CHAPTER V.

1. *The Futility of Seeking Justification by Legal Works,* 2-12.—To receive circumcision as being necessary to salvation is a virtual renunciation of Christ (2). When one submits to this rite as a condition of justification, he thereby commits himself to the legal method, and, by the very meaning of his act, is bound to do all that the law requires and must do this, if he is to be saved (3). You Galatians, in so doing, are cutting your life loose from Christ by renouncing the faith-principle of salvation and are already turned away from God's free grace in the attempt to achieve your own salvation by works of merit (4). I assure you of your great error, and certain failure, for we who hold to the opposite course base all our hope upon the grace in which we trust (5); and rightly so, for, with reference to the attainment of salvation, the question whether one is circumcised or not, is of no importance; the only essential condition being a faith which gives evidence of its vital power by love (6).

Analysis and Paraphrase of Chapter V.

You were making good progress in Christian life and knowledge; who has checked you in this and led you into such disloyalty to the truth? Their dissuasion of you from the right path is not in line with God's call. This wrong tendency is indeed serious, for, though the defection be limited, it will spread like leaven (7-8). I have good hope, however, that you Galatians as a whole will not be led astray by this error, but will continue faithful to my instructions; but the leader in this sedition will receive a heavy chastisement (10). As for the accusation of the Judaizers that I too, upon occasion, preach circumcision, it involves an absurdity; they would not continue to persecute me if I were not in antagonism to them; if their accusation were true, there would no longer be any offence to the Jews from my preaching of the cross; but the fact that my work still arouses Jewish opposition, proves their charge untrue. These extremists who pervert your faith and hinder your Christian growth,—who think so much of circumcision—should have it to the point of mutilation! (11, 12).

2. *The right use of Christian freedom*, 13-15.—I speak thus vehemently, for you, Christian brethren, were destined (in your divine call) for the enjoyment of freedom from these legal requirements; but this freedom does not mean lawlessness, but requires a loving service to others; for love to one's fellows as to himself is the sum of the law for

196 *Analysis and Paraphrase of Chapter V.*

which you profess so much zeal, (13, 14). But if, instead of living the life of love, you continue in disputes, such as that now prevailing, you will end in the utter destruction of your Christian fellowship (15).

3. *The Spiritual and the Carnal life contrasted*, 16-26.—My advice is: Live under the power of the Spirit and, in so doing, you will find the true safeguard against the evils of which I warn you (16). For there is a sharp conflict in Christian men between the inspiration of the Spirit and the sinful impulses which operate to prevent your doing what your conscience would prompt (17). But if you keep your lives under the guidance of the Spirit you shall have the victory over evil, because you will not then be under that condemnation and bondage which they experience who live under the law, but will enjoy the sense of freedom and pardon which the Spirit imparts (18). Now by considering the sins which spring from carnal impulse, you may see how wholly incompatible they are with participation in the kingdom of God (19-21), and by contemplating the fruit in human life of the Spirit's guidance, it is equally seen that those who produce it cannot be under the bondage of sin and the sentence of the law, since those virtues are the ideal requirements of all law (22, 23). Now Christians have put to death the impulses which lead to the works of the

flesh (24). If, then, we have our life in the power of the Spirit and not of the flesh, let our outward action be ruled by the true power of Christian living—that of the Spirit; let us not act as if we were ruled by the contrary and inconsistent principle which excites factious boasting leading to the challenging of one another to conflicts and to jealous retaliation (25, 26).

CHAPTER V.

1. With freedom did Christ set us free: stand fast therefore, and be not entangled in a yoke of bondage. This verse logically belongs in connection with the preceding section. The text is well nigh hopelessly undetermined and the precise force intended not certain, whichever reading is chosen.* The general sense, however, cannot be in doubt. "Ye Christians are no longer

---

* For an account of the various readings in the original text, see Lightfoot's Excursus in his Commentary, page 200 seq. The preferred reading (so ℵ A. B. C. D. et al.) is: τῇ ἐλευθερίᾳ ἡμᾶς Χρ. ἠλ., (so Westcott and Hort, Meyer, Tischendorf). If the relative ᾗ is thus omitted, τῇ ἐλευθερίᾳ is to be joined with the verb, ἠλευθέρωσεν, and the meaning is either: "With freedom did Christ set us free:" *i. e.* ᾗ is a dative of means (so R. V. text); or: "For freedom did Christ set us free," *i. e.* ᾗ is a dative *commodi*, (so R. V. margin, Lightfoot, [in case the text is to be so written] Meyer). All things considered, this last meaning seems to be the most natural sense of the passage, though by no means free from difficulty and objection. If ᾗ is read (so Lightfoot, Ellicott), then τῇ ἐλευθερίᾳ, may be connected either with what precedes (Lightfoot) and a period placed

under the guilt and curse of the law. Make the most of the fact and stand boldly forth as the representatives of the liberty from sin which is yours," is the Apostle's meaning.

II. THE FUTILITY OF SEEKING JUSTIFICATION BY LEGAL WORKS, 2-12.

2. Behold, I Paul say unto you, that, if ye receive circumcision, Christ will profit you nothing.—As a reason for his exhortation Paul now asserts the mutually exclusive character of the systems of law and grace. If one commits himself to the law-system by circumcision, he cannot be, at the same time, an adherent of the grace-system. One cannot hold these contradictory opposites in respect to the mode of justification and the conditions of salvation, at the same time. Paul will sharply set before them the alternative. He will present this alternative sharply to every person by the use of **Behold** in a singular (form ἴδε) and by appealing to them individ-

---

after ἠλευθέρωσεν, or with στήκετε (A. V. Ellicott); a construction which would yield two possible meanings (a) = ἐν τῇ ἐλευθ. (A. V.), or (b) τῇ ἐλευθ. might be dative of respect, *quod attinet ad libertatem* (Ellicott), and ᾗ in that case can be taken either instrumentally (A. V.) "wherewith:" or as dative *commodi* (Ellicott) "for which Christ hath made us free."

ually (παντὶ ἀνθρώπῳ, ver. 3). He introduces his own name to add to his warning the solemn emphasis of his Apostolic authority. His argument is: "If you become circumcised then you deliberately commit yourselves to the law-system and renounce the benefits of the gracious system; you are then seeking salvation on your own merits, a proceeding which, by its very nature, shuts you out from the acceptance of God's grace by faith." His meaning cannot be that circumcision in itself is a barrier to Christian salvation, for neither circumcision nor uncircumcision, is anything in itself (v. 6; vi. 15), from the point of view of Christian salvation. On the contrary, the meaning is: "If you by circumcision espouse the old system as necessary to salvation,"—as the whole course of the argument shows.

3. Yea, I testify again to every man that receiveth circumcision, that he is a debtor to do the whole law.—"Yea (δὲ) in that case," continues the Apostle, "so far will you be from receiving profit of Christ that you will find yourselves under all the burdens of debt which the law imposes." **Again** probably refers back to similar warnings given them when he visited them. To every person who thus chooses the law-method, he again bears testimony that such a one is a debtor to keep the whole law. The law is a unit, and it is vain to suppose that any one of its requirements (as circumcision) is necessary to salvation, and not all. He will not succeed in attaining justification on the legal basis, unless he attain complete obedience. If they will appeal from Christ to Moses, to Moses they shall go.

4. Ye are severed from Christ, ye who would be justified by the law; ye are fallen away from grace:—Severed from (κατηργήθητε ἀπὸ Χρ.)—lit. "destroyed or made nothing from," a *constructio pregnans* (= καταργεῖσθαι καὶ χωρίζεσθαι ἀπό). See also Rom. vii: 2–6 where the dissolution of the relation of the Christian to the law is referred to. The meaning is: "Ye are wholly separated from Christ ye who are such as (οἵτινες) to be justified by the law. The present tense, "*receiveth* circumcision," v. 3, and "are justified, (R. V. "would be justified") (περιτεμνομένω, δικαιοῦσθε) refer to the effort now making by the Judaizers to have recourse to the law-principle in seeking salvation. **Ye are fallen away from grace**, lit. "ye fell out from grace," (τῆς χάριτος ἐξεπέσατε). The past tense (Aorist) is used in reference to the time when they committed themselves to the effort which they are now making, *i. e.* by appealing to the law they adopt the principle of salvation by works instead of salvation by grace. They have thus fallen away from the plane of grace down upon the debit and credit basis where they find themselves powerless to pay their obligations.

Paul here speaks as if this desertion of Christ were an accomplished fact, but other expressions show that he was not yet without hope of reclaiming these misguided Galatians. The completed lapse seems to have been logically rather than actually accomplished. Their position that circumcision was necessary to salvation had not yet led them to perceive that this position involved the giving up of Christ as Saviour. Paul's purpose was to warn them by pointing out the inevitable consequence to which this position must lead. Already their attitude logically separated them from Christ; it had not actually done so in most cases; certainly not consciously to themselves.

5. For we through the Spirit by faith wait for the hope of righteousness.—This verse and the next introduce the Christian principle by way of contrast to the law-principle and thus confirm the mutual exclusiveness of the two. "For we, on our part, by the (Holy) Spirit (which we received through the hearing of faith, iii. 2) eagerly expect the hope of righteousness as the result of faith." Here are presented two ideas regarding the mode of salvation: (*a*) It is through the agency of the Spirit; (*b*) It is from faith, as the condition, on man's part, of apprehending the grace offered.

The expression: **We wait for the hope of righteousness,** points forward to the completed salvation in the future life. The hope of righteous-

No Justification by Legal Works: v. 6. 203

ness (ἐλπίδα δικαιοσύνης) probably means: The hope of being declared righteous at the last judgment. It is thus the hope which terminates upon and is fulfilled in, the declared acceptance with God, (*i. e.* δικαιοσύνης, genitive of the object). Others interpret thus: We await the hope (the fulfillment of the hope) which springs from and is warranted by our justification thus making δικ. subjective genitive.

6. For in Christ Jesus neither circumcision availeth anything, nor uncircumcision ; but faith working through love.— This statement is confirmatory (γάρ) of the principle that the hope of righteousness is born of faith and based upon grace. An outward rite like circumcision counts for nothing in itself in God's judgment, nor can it as a symbol of attachment to the law, have saving significance, because the law itself is rendered powerless to save by the flesh (Rom. viii. 3). Hence this door of hope is shut; there remains only the way of faith. "But in saying faith," says Paul, "I mean an active and energetic faith."* This passage shows how far Paul is from employing faith in the sense of dead and inactive belief,—the meaning of the term against which James inveighs (Jas.

---

* Ἐνεργουμένη is middle, not passive, and active in force (as always in the New Testament; *e. g.* II Cor. i. 6; I Thess. ii. 13).

ii. 14–26). Faith is an energetic principle which is active in the sphere of love; *i. e.* which leads to good works in the sense in which James commends them. Vv. 7–9 contain a warning to the Galatian Christians against the Judaizers; 10–12, a severe censure of those who have led them astray.

7. Ye were running well; who did hinder you that ye should not obey the truth?—Ye were running well, *i. e.*, growing and prospering in the Christian life. **Who did hinder,** etc., (τίς ὑμᾶς ἐνέκοψεν), is the rhetorical question expressing surprise. Some one has impeded you in your course of obeying the truth. By **the truth** here is meant the doctrine of the sole saving efficacy of faith.

8. This persuasion came not of him that calleth you.—The word rendered **persuasion** here (πεισμονή) is apparently chosen with reference to the verb meaning to obey (πείθεσθαι) in the previous verse, thus making a paronomasia. The meaning seems to be: "This dissuasion (active) from the truth of the gospel emanates not from him who calls you, *i. e.*, from God. It is hostile to the divine purpose and requirement for your Christian lives." Many understand "persuasion" in a passive sense: "the compliance which you have accorded to these teachers," but that meaning does not seem to agree so well with the phrase, **of him that calleth you.** Still others render, "credulity;" others, "obstinacy;" others, "self-confidence." But the choice lies between the first two. Meyer, Ellicott and Thayer's Lexicon take the word in an active sense.

9. A little leaven leaveneth the whole lump.—To the assurance that the persuasion to still cling to the law is evil and perilous, Paul applies the maxim concerning the spread of evil which likens it to leaven. Probably the basis of the maxim was the Levitical defilement occasioned by leaven which necessitated its removal from the house before the Passover. The same figure occurs in I Cor. v. 7; Mark viii. 15. Whether the doctrines or the persons of the Judaizers are meant by leaven is probably a fruitless dispute, since, if it is their doctrines, it is these as made effectual by personal effort; and, if it is the persons, it is they as teaching certain doctrines.

10. I have confidence to you-ward in the Lord, that ye will be none otherwise minded: but he that troubleth you shall bear his judgment, whosoever he be.—Here the Apostle adopts a more hopeful and confident tone, which shows that he did not regard the Galatians as having actually reached the pitch of apostasy described, but rather as having entered the way which, if continued in, would inevitably lead to it. He has confidence in respect to them in the Lord that they will not be otherwise minded; *i. e.*, otherwise than his warnings and advice would require. His vehemence is directed rather against the Judaizing false teachers and their principles, than against the Galatian church as such. He believes that they will be recovered out of their peril. The troubler (whoever he is),—a quite general expression, as if Paul did not wish to personally specify even if he knew who he was,—shall bear his judgment. Some person who had been chiefly influential in producing the schism is evidently in the writer's mind.

11. But I, brethren, if I still preach circumcision, why am I still persecuted? then hath the stumblingblock of the cross been done away.—The mention of these errorists calls to mind their charge or assertion that he (Paul) at other times and places so far agreed with them as to preach circumcision. They might appeal to the circumcision of Timothy (Acts xvi. 3), or, possibly, to such principles as that of Paul: "To the Jews I became as a Jew" (I Cor. ix. 20), which apparently led to his taking the vow and shaving his head at Cenchreæ (Acts xviii. 18). "But how absurd!" exclaims Paul, "as if I would continue to suffer persecution for a principle which I do not think important enough to always and consistently maintain." His persecution was just because of his opposition to the law as a means of salvation. There would be no occasion for such persecution if this assertion were true. "Then were the offense of the cross done away;" that is, if it were true that I continue to preach circumcision, then the Jews ought to cease to persecute me for preaching the cross instead of the law, for then I should really be on their side and the offensive doctrine of the cross need no longer provoke their persecutions.

12. I would that they which unsettle you would even cut themselves off.—The thought of such false charges from his opponents now wrings from Paul this bitterly satirical wish. They think so much of circumcision that they falsify my teaching to support their view of it. They ought to have it to the point of mutilation.*

II. THE RIGHT USE OF CHRISTIAN FREEDOM, 13-15.

13. For ye, brethren, were called for freedom; only use not your freedom for an occasion to the flesh, but through love be servants one to another.—In contrast with the bondage into which circumcision leads, stands the liberty to which the Christian is called. The

---

* Such is the meaning of 'ἀποκόπτομαι (and not "excommunicate ") as most interpreters now agree. Septuagint usage in similar connections (cf. Deut. xxiii. 1) confirms this view. The verb is reflexive middle, and the καί designates this action as something beyond circumcision: "*even* do this."

for gives the ground for Paul's strong denunciation of those who would lead the Galatian Christians into bondage. "Well, may I rebuke them, *for* (γάρ) they would prevent the realization of the very idea of Christian calling, which is that of liberty." **For** (ἐπί) **freedom,** lit. "on the ground of freedom, on the plane of freedom,"—so that freedom is the characteristic of your calling,—and thus the preposition comes to denote the moral end in view. **Only use not,** etc., introduces a caution against misunderstanding this doctrine of liberty: "Do not understand that liberty involves license. Freedom from the Mosaic law is not equivalent to freedom from moral law or constraints. You are freed from its curse, but are under Christ's law, the highest of all moral requirements," etc.

The flesh (τῇ σαρκί), in an ethical sense, as opposed to love and service. Compare the "works of the flesh," ver. 19 *seq*. They are under Christ's law of love and service which forms the sharpest contrast to the freedom of license.

14. For the whole law is fulfilled in one word, even in this; Thou shalt love thy neighbor as thyself.—This verse is explanatory of that serving of one another in love which was just commended. **The whole law** is the whole Mosaic law. They are still under its essential content of moral requirement because that is taken up into Christianity as the law of love; they

Spiritual and Carnal Life Contrasted: v. 15.

are not under the Mosaic system *as such*, but are under the law of love, which was, indeed, an element of that system. **Is fulfilled,** *i. e.* "stands fulfilled" (πεπλήρωται), denoting a present and permanent fact. Compliance with the law of love, which Christianity requires, is the fulfillment of the ideal content of the Mosaic system. Christianity has taken up this ideal content and fully developed and fulfilled it; each person, therefore, who obeys that law of love as taught by Christ fulfils the law personally. Love is the all-comprehending principle which embraces the moral ends which the Mosaic law was designed to serve.

15. But if ye bite and devour one another, take heed that ye be not consumed one of another:—But if, forsaking this law, **ye bite and devour one another,** in party strife, such as those heretical teachers engender, you will end by destroying each other as a Christian community. Love is the only true bond of fellowship. If you resort to selfish strife and censorious treatment of each other, your common Christian life will be rendered impossible. That spirit destroys Christian society.

III. THE SPIRITUAL AND THE CARNAL LIFE CONTRASTED, 16–26.

16. But I say, Walk by the Spirit, and ye shall not fulfil the lust of the flesh.—

We now have a fuller exposition of these two contrasted courses of life: love and selfish strife. **But I say,** that is, this is what I mean: **Walk by the Spirit,** by the aid of the Holy Spirit who sheds abroad in the heart the love of God, **and ye** (certainly) **shall not** (note the double negative οὐ μή with the Aorist subjunctive) **fulfil,** etc. The two courses are contrary, and if you follow the true one, you will thereby be protected against the false.

17. For the flesh lusteth against the Spirit, and the Spirit against the flesh; for these are contrary the one to the other; that ye may not do the things that ye would.—He further explains the mutually exclusive character of these two modes of life; they are irreconcilable in principle,—the flesh and the Spirit,—or love, issuing in service (ver. 13), and selfishness issuing in strife and hatred (ver. 15), are contrary. There is a zeugma here. The verb **lusteth** (ἐπιθυμεῖ), could not in strict propriety be predicated of the Spirit. The meaning is, the carnal desires are contrary to the Spirit, and the impulses from the Spirit are contrary to these desires. That **Spirit** here is the Holy Spirit, not man's own spirit, is rendered almost certain by such analogous passages as Rom. viii. 9, 11, 14; Gal. iii. 2, 5; iv. 6. **That ye may not,** etc., (ἵνα μή κ. τ. λ.) has here the full telic force. It is the *purpose* of this opposition on the part of each principle, that men should not follow the other. The flesh is opposed to the Spirit in order to secure the result that men should not do what they wish, so far as they may be aiming and striving to follow the Spirit; and the Spirit opposes the flesh in order to secure the result that men do not what they wish, so far as they wish to follow the flesh. In saying **the things that ye would,** Paul is thinking of the will as for the time identified with the principle against which the active opposition is at any time made by the opposing principle. Thus: The Spirit strives to hinder your following the flesh when you desire to do so; and the flesh tries to hinder your following the Spirit when you wish to do that. No onesided interpretation of the phrase, (*e. g.* by defining it as the "carnal will," or the "moral will,") should be adopted.

18. But if ye are led by the Spirit, ye are not under the law.—Here the opposition of principles seems almost to be between the Spirit and the law. It is so in this sense: If ye are led by the Spirit then you have freedom and newness of life, and are not under the condemnation of the law which your carnal lives brought upon you. The opposition is not strictly between the Spirit and the law *as such,* but between being led by the Spirit and the condition of condemnation under the law. It is a contrast of two human conditions: that in which men are led by the Spirit, and that of being under the law. The common interpretation:

Being led by the Spirit you have the law in your hearts, etc., and hence are not under it, yields an idea correct and important in itself, but not the primary thought here intended.

19. Now the works of the flesh are manifest, which are these, fornication, uncleanness, lasciviousness.—The two modes of life are now pictured by their operations and effects. From the enumeration of the **works of the flesh** (τὰ ἔργα τῆς σαρκός), we see that the **flesh** (σάρξ) must be used in an ethical, and not in a physical, sense. The first three (**fornication, uncleanness, lasciviousness**), are carnal sins.

20. Idolatry, sorcery, enmities, strife, jealousies, wraths, factions, divisions, heresies.—The next two (**idolatry, sorcery**) are connected especially with false religions. The next four (**enmities, strife, jealousies, wraths**) are evil passions. The next three (**factions, divisions, heresies**) denote certain social effects which spring from evil passions.

21. Envyings, drunkenness, revellings, and such like: of the which I forewarn you, even as I did forewarn you, that they which practice such things shall not inherit the kingdom of God:—Envyings seem to belong logically with the group beginning: **Enmities,** and then follows the mention of such outbreaking sins as **drunkenness** and **revel-**

lings. The phrase **kingdom of God** seems to be used eschatologically here, but it does not seem probable that (with Meyer) **they which practice such things** (τοιαῦτα πράσσοντες), should be understood to refer to Christians who by doing these things had forfeited the kingdom. The inference is rather that such persons may not enter the kingdom, because they have nothing in common with its principles and truths.

22. But the fruit of the Spirit is love, joy, peace, longsuffering, kindness, goodness, faithfulness.—Observe the use of the singular **fruit** (καρπός),—rather than the plural—to denote the idea of internal unity and moral homogeneity (so Meyer); but no good reason for the change from the term **works** (ἔργα) to **fruit** can be given, except variety. No special logical arrangement seems intended among these nine virtues.

23. Meekness, temperance: against such there is no law.—Against them there is no law; therefore there can be no condemnation to those who possess these qualities. To be led by the Spirit means to possess and cultivate these qualities, and those who are so led are not under law because there is no law against the character which they possess. **Such** (τοιούτων) is, most probably, neuter, and not masculine (as is frequently held), and refers to the virtues enumerated above.

24. And they that are of Christ Jesus

have crucified the flesh with the passions and the lusts thereof:—Have crucified, more exactly, **crucified** (ἐσταύρωσαν). The Aorist most naturally refers to the time when they became Christians; *cf.* "We who died to sin," Rom. vi. 2; "I am crucified with Christ," Gal. ii. 20; "Buried with him through baptism," Rom. vi. 4. The death, resurrection and glorification of Christ yield a terminology which is used in an ethical sense in application to the believer in his Christian life. The crucifixion of the flesh is the renouncing of the life of sin whose seat is in the flesh, so that as Christ was crucified objectively, so the Christian should, in a moral sense, crucify, that is, put to death the flesh, so as to render its sinful impulses ineffective. The **passions** (παθήματα) are the affections which give rise to the feelings called **lusts** (ἐπιθυμίαι).

25. If we live by the Spirit, by the Spirit let us also walk.—The inner *life* and outward *conduct* should correspond. **By the Spirit** (in both cases dative of instrument, as in verse 16): If our inner, spiritual life is sustained by the power of the Spirit, we should also walk by his aid and according to his guidance.

26. Let us not be vainglorious, provoking one another, envying one another.—This is the concluding exhortation. "Desirous of vain glory," (κενόδοξοι),—a reference to the spirit of rivalry and jealousy which Pharisaic influences had awakened and developed among them, (*cf.* ver. 15); **provoking** or "challenging one another" (ἀλλήλους παρακαλούμενοι), referring to strifes of opinion in the hope of triumphing over the rival party; **envying one another** (ἀλλήλοις φθονοῦντες), that is, cherishing grudges against those whom, perhaps, they would not openly challenge to party strife.

ANALYSIS AND PARAPHRASE OF CHAPTER VI.

1. *The Nature and Obligation of the Christian Law of Love,* 1–5.—Brethren, if sin overtake one of your number, you who are guided by the Spirit should correct the fault and restore the man in a temper of gentleness, remembering that you too may be similarly tempted and may need a similar forgiveness (1). The true law which you are to obey is that of Christ which requires you, through love, to share the cares and sorrows of others (2). For if, on the contrary, one cultivates the opposite spirit of pride and self-sufficiency, he exercises a perverted moral judgment and is self-deceived (3). Each man stands for himself and not by comparison with others. Let him, therefore, test his own actions on their own merits, for each must bear his own burden of responsibility and accountability (4, 5).

2. *The Law of the Spiritual Harvest,* 6–10.— Those who receive Christian instruction should permit their teachers to share in the good things which God has given them (6). Do not deceive

Analysis and Paraphrase of Chapter VI. 217

yourselves by thinking that you can shun this obligation of love; God does not submit to the mockery attempted by those who think they may escape the just consequences of their actions; he that lives and acts in accord with the natural, selfish impulses shall incur the consequence,—a corrupted moral life, while he who lives under the guidance of the Holy Spirit shall attain the goal of an incorruptible existence (7, 8). Let this law of the spiritual harvest encourage us to right-doing, for our reward is secure; let us, accordingly, faithfully discharge our obligations to all men, remembering those special duties which we owe to Christian brethren (9, 10).

3. *The True Ground of Glorying*, 11-18.—Observe with what large (misshapen) letters I have written this Epistle with my own hand (betokening my great concern for you which overcame my hesitation from inexperience in writing; See Introduction (II) and notes), (1). To sum up: Those who are constraining you to be circumcised are thereby but displaying their zeal for carnal ordinances; their aim is to escape those persecutions from the Jews which they would suffer if, like myself, they avowed their adherence solely to the doctrine of the cross (12). They are themselves not consistent in observing the law, but they are anxious to have you circumcised that they may make a great show of zeal for the Jewish religion by having won you Gentiles to its observance (13). But, as for me, I

218 *Analysis and Paraphrase of Chapter VI.*

disclaim all grounds of glorying except the cross of Christ by which (so R. V., see notes) I have broken off all relations to the sinful world as if by death (14). Since Christ's death is the true saving power, I am indifferent to the question of circumcision (in itself) and make newness of life through Christ my great concern (15). This truth (the importance of renewed life) supplies the rule and test of action and belief. Peace and mercy be upon all such (who will thereby prove themselves the true Israelites) as adopt and obey it! (16). Let me not be troubled more by these errors and accusations, for the proof that I am Christ's is found in the scars upon my body which I have received in his service. Grace be with you (17, 18).

CHAPTER VI.

I. THE NATURE AND OBLIGATION OF THE CHRISTIAN LAW OF LOVE, 1-5.

AFTER administering the severe rebukes to the Galatians which we have studied, the Apostle takes a more conciliatory tone. He reminds them that, though some have been led astray into faults and errors, they are not to reject but rather to restore them. The lack of any praise at the beginning of the letter is partially compensated by this kindly and gentle closing, beginning with a fraternal address.

1. Brethren, even if a man be overtaken in any trespass, ye which are spiritual, restore such a one in a spirit of meekness; looking to thyself, lest thou also be tempted:—Even if (ἐὰν καί), more exactly: "if even," or "although;" if a man be *even overtaken* by a fault, which pursues him faster than he can escape (so Meyer, Ellicott). The word **even** (καί) "points to an aggravated offense" (Ellicott). Others interpret **overtaken** (προλημφθῇ) as meaning "to be caught by it before one fairly sees it," that is, "to be surprised by it," (so Lightfoot). In either case, the preposition **in** (ἐν) conveys the idea of one's being held in it, caught in its grasp or power. **In any trespass** or transgression (παράπτωμα); no doubt said with special reference to the lapse of the Galatians from Christian faith and life under the leading of the Jewish errorists, but yet left quite general so as to be a comprehensive statement of principle. **Ye which are spiritual** (οἱ πνευματικοί) those who are led by the Holy Spirit (πνεῦμα ἅγιον) as opposed to the "natural" (ψυχικοί) I Cor. ii. 14, or "carnal" (σαρκικοί) I Cor. iii. 1-4. In Rom. xv. 1 we have a kindred contrast of the "strong" (δυνατοί) and "weak" (ἀδύνατοι). Paul leaves each person to decide to which class he belongs, in accordance with the definitions of the "spiritual" and the "carnal" life which he has given, (the walking κατὰ πνεῦμα, or κατὰ σάρκα). **Restore** (καταρτίζετε), lit. "adjust," "set right," that is, bring back to their true normal Christian life. **A spirit of meekness** (πνεῦμα πραΰτητος) is undertood by Luther, Calvin, Lightfoot, De Wette, Wieseler *et al.* to denote a certain tone or temper of the human spirit. Meyer regards it as a designation of the Holy Spirit (as also in I Cor. iv. 21). But in this passage the phrase is correlative to "in love" (ἐν ἀγάπῃ), a fact which strongly favors the meaning: "in a *temper* of meekness." The primary reference seems clearly to be to that temper whereby they prove themselves to be spiritual, and thus the reference is, indirectly, to the Holy Spirit, so far as this grace of meekness is a fruit of his indwelling, (so Ellicott). **Looking to thyself** (σκοπῶν σεαυτόν); he here changes to the singular number and individualizes the thought: "taking heed each of you;" **lest thou also be tempted,** drawn by temptation into the sins of the unspiritual, and thus fall into the same need of sympathy and help which it is now your duty to render in the case of the fallen one just spoken of.

2. Bear ye one another's burdens, and so fulfil the law of Christ.—The bearing of burdens here refers primarily to such a possible fall as is alluded to in verse 1. **Bear,** that is, take on thyself, sympathize with,—the condition precedent of all successful efforts to free one from those burdens. **And so fulfil,** etc.* The law of Christ is the law of love, and it is the nature of love by sympathy to bear the burdens of its object. Perhaps in

---

* Most recent texts here read the future indicative (ἀναπληρώσετε) instead of the Aorist imperative (ἀναπληρώσατε) of the older editions. (So Meyer, Lightfoot, Ellicott, Tischendorf; *per contra*, Westcott and Hort, R. V.) The meaning is more pointed and forcible if the future is read. "Do this and then you will fulfil Christ's law." The fulfillment is accomplished in the bearing of burdens; that *is* the fulfillment.

the word **law** here there is a side reference to the Galatians' *legal* tendencies. "If you will obey the law," says the Apostle, "this is the law, viz., *love.*" It is the law of Christ both as *given*, and as perfectly *illustrated*, by Christ, (*cf.* Matt. viii. 17). The meaning of **burdens** (βάρη) can be legitimately extended in idea so as to embrace "infirmities" (ἀσθενήματα, Rom. xv. 1), though the primary reference is to cases of lapse into error and consequent unfaithfulness to Christ.

3. For if a man thinketh himself to be something, when he is nothing, he deceiveth himself.—A contrast with the two preceding verses is now introduced. If, instead of helping others in a spirit of meekness, and bearing their burdens, which involves humility and unselfishness, the opposite spirit is cherished, the Christian deceives himself by supposing that he is morally something when he is nothing. If one thinks that he is so great that he cannot stoop to service, then he is, when morally judged, simply nothing, and his self-esteem is self-deception. The true greatness of the Christian is found, where Christ's greatness was found, in service and usefulness. He that is above it in his own conceit, is wholly below it in fact, and hence **deceiveth himself,** (φρεναπατᾷ ἑαυτόν),—he practices a mental and moral deception upon himself.

4. But let each man prove his own

work, and then shall he have his glorying in regard of himself alone, and not of his neighbor.—But, as opposed to this vain course of self-esteem and self-deception, **let each man prove,** etc. (δοκιμάζετω, κ. τ. λ.) that is, put his work to the test, to see whether it is real and genuine, to discover what are the real motives and principles out of which it springs. **His own work** (τὸ ἔργον ἑαυτοῦ); **work** is used in a collective sense, as including his whole life and conduct. And then he shall have a ground of boasting (καύχημα) with reference to himself, and not with reference to his neighbor; *i. e.*, he shall have a real ground of rejoicing by reason of the value and genuineness of his own work, and not merely with reference to some one else's work. It will be *in re, non in collatione* (Castalio). The "ground of boasting" of the one who thinks he is something when he is nothing, is the false and vain glorying of one who fancies himself superior to others. It has no real and valid basis, as it does in the case of the man who puts his work to the test of the gospel of love and burden-bearing (*cf.* II Cor. x. 12).

5. For each man shall bear his own burden.—This saying sharpens and confirms the contrast between the true glorying in regard to one's own work (εἰς ἑαυτόν), and not merely by contrast with others (εἰς τὸν ἕτερον). The argument is: You should test your work and have a basis of rejoicing in your own work, for every one must bear his own burden (or "load," φορτίον) of responsibility, and, if his work does not stand the test, his burden of blame. We cannot escape the obligations connected with our own work, and no one else can carry them for us. There is here only a verbal, not a real, disharmony with verse 2. There we have a command; here a statement of fact. There burdens of sin and sorrow are meant; here burdens of responsibility. There, the maxim is urged as a proof of being spiritual; here the law of individual responsibility is laid down as an explanation of the moral testing which comes to every life.

THE LAW OF THE SPIRITUAL HARVEST, 6-10.

6. But let him that is taught in the word communicate unto him that teacheth in all good things:—Is taught (κατηχούμενος); the verb literally means, "to sound down" (into the ears), applied, *e. g.* to the instruction proceeding from the teacher to the child; in the passive, to be instructed (*cf.* Luke i. 4). From this verb we have our word "Catechumen." Of the verse, as a whole, there are two interpretations: (1) **Let him that is taught,** that is, the hearer, the church-member, communicate, have something in common with him that teaches, the Christian preacher, meaning, "Let the church support its ministers." Here **all good things** refers to worldly goods, and **communicate** refers to the impartation of these to the Christian teachers, (so Lightfoot, Ellicott, De Wette, Olshausen, Wieseler). (2) "Let the disciple have fellowship with the teacher in everything morally good" (Meyer). The terms used by the Apostle are quite general, and can hardly be said to refer explicitly to the support of the ministry; but the habit of Paul in freely mentioning the duty of giving, makes it probable that he had this in mind here. In either case, the verse urges the duty of fellowship as contrasted with that selfish isolation of those who falsely "think themselves to be something."

7. Be not deceived; God is not mocked: for whatsoever a man soweth, that shall he also reap.—The thought is: Do not think that you can evade these duties and obligations. Do not deceive yourselves. God is not mocked, does not suffer himself to be mocked, as if one could omit his obligation, and, escaping notice, taunt the divine Being with having overlooked his omission. That can never be. None can escape God's order or his law. The relation between action and judgment is inevitable, and this is proof that God does not permit himself to be mocked.

8. For he that soweth unto his own flesh shall of the flesh reap corruption; but he that soweth unto the Spirit shall of the Spirit reap eternal life.—These words are designed to illustrate the principle that we reap what we sow. In verse 7 two opposite kinds of seed are thought of; here opposite kinds of recipient soil, *i.e.* the **flesh** (σάρξ) and the **spirit** (πνεῦμα). The meaning is: "He who acts with reference to the flesh, whose life is determined by the natural impulses and desires, rather than by the divine law of love, shall reap 'corruption,'—the opposite of eternal life; not physical corruption, which comes to all, but moral corruption or destruction, the death of the soul as opposed to its true life. He that sows unto the Spirit, whose life is determined and guided by the Spirit, shall attain eternal life."

9. And let us not be weary in well-doing: for in due season we shall reap, if we faint not.—"As opposed to the carnal life whose end is loss of soul, let us not lose heart in well-doing." The figure of labor in sowing is still carried out. Let us keep on sowing "unto the Spirit," for we have the encouragement that we shall reap, at the time destined for reaping. Luther has this apt comment on the words: "It is an easy matter for a man to do good once or twice; but to continue and not to be discouraged through the ingratitude and perverseness of those to whom he hath done good, that is very hard. Therefore he doth not only exhort us to do good, but also not to be weary in doing good. As if he said: Wait and look for the perfected harvest that is to come and then shall no ingratitude or perverse dealing of men be able to pluck you away from well-doing; for in the harvest time ye shall receive most plentiful increase and proof of your seed. Thus with the most sweet words he exhorteth the faithful to the doing of good works."

10. So then, as we have opportunity, let us work that which is good toward all men, and especially toward them that are of the household of the faith:—So then, as a conclusion from the certainty of our reaping if we faint not, when we have a favoring time, **opportunity** (καιρόν), **let us work,** etc. **That which is good** (τὸ ἀγαθόν) is "the true, moral, Christian good." **Them that are of the household** (οἱ οἰκεῖοι) are the members of the Christian family, whose bond of union is faith. Our duty is to minister to the true good of all, but there are special obligations between those who have the common bond of faith, as there are special obligations between members of the same family, to serve each other.

THE TRUE GROUND OF GLORYING, 11–18.

11. See with how large letters I have written unto you with mine own hand.— The A. V. is certainly wrong in rendering: "Ye see how large a letter I have written," as if the reference were to the length of the Epistle. The student of the original text will note that the Apostle does not use the word for an "epistle" (ἐπιστολή), but that which refers to letters of the alphabet (γράμματα), and that it is dative plural, denoting means. Paul was accustomed to write the closing verses of his Epistles (cf. II Thess. iii. 17; I Cor. xvi. 21), containing his own and, perhaps, other salutations, while the body of the letter was written by an amanuensis (Rom. xvi. 22).

There are two views of the phrase (rendered in R. V.): **I have written** (ἔγραψα): (1) Epistolary aorist. "I wrote,"—thought of from the point of time when it should be read (cf. Philemon 19) (so Meyer, Lightfoot). (2) It refers to the writing of the whole epistle which Paul had written with his own hand (if so, it is the only known case of the kind, except, perhaps, the private letter to Philemon, cf. verse 19). It is certain that the epistolary aorist *usually* refers, in Paul's writings, to what has gone before, either in some other letter (I Cor. v. 9), or to a foregoing part of the letter in writing (I Cor. ix. 15), and, in the view of many, it is so in all cases (so Ewald, Ellicott, Wieseler). This view appears to me preferable. Many take **how large** (πηλίκοις) to mean large and bungling, because he was unaccustomed to writing Greek. Meyer interprets: "Written large for emphasis." * All things con-

---

* In Meyer's view the reason for the emphasis is, that in these concluding verses, he sums up the most important points of the Epistle, and wishes to call special attention to them by the large hand in which they are written.

sidered, the verse seems to imply that Paul wrote the whole letter with characters unusually large, probably from inexpertness or lack of practice in the writing of Greek; possibly because "more accustomed to the use of a tool than a pen" (Weiss).

12. As many as desire to make a fair show in the flesh, they compel you to be circumcised; only that they may not be persecuted for the cross of Christ.—He now commences a summing up of the main points in controversy, considering first the spirit and effect of the Judaizers' teaching. The first charge against them is, that they wish to make a display of their religion in outward ordinances. **In the flesh,** that is, in the sphere to which circumcision belongs; in outward observances as opposed to spiritual life and service. They wish to show fair, to be punctilious and zealous in this sphere, so as to put on an appearance of much religious earnestness. But this apparent religious zeal is really selfish and hypocritical. They urge you to be circumcised only that they may not incur the dislike of the Jews, and so be compelled to suffer persecution. If they espoused the doctrine of the cross as teaching the one true way of salvation, the Jews would persecute them. This they avoid by a pretence of great devotion to the Jewish law, as when they insist upon the necessity of circumcision. According to Meyer, **in the flesh** here means "the sinful nature of man," and describes rather the inward life-element in which they are striving to make a fair show, than the outward sphere in which they choose to make the effort. The term **the flesh** usually has this ethical sense in Paul's writings, and always when used in direct contrast with "the Spirit," but I am inclined, from the reference in the context to circumcision, and from the phrase, "in your flesh" (verse 13), where the reference is to circumcision, to give the word here the meaning of the outward sphere as opposed to the spiritual realm. (So Thayer's Lexicon; *cf.* Phil. iii. 3, 4). The second charge against the Judaizers is, then, that their religious zeal for circumcision has in it the prudential motive of escaping persecution on account of the doctrine of the cross for which they would be persecuted if they preached it.

13. For not even they who receive circumcision do themselves keep the law; but they desire to have you circumcised, that they may glory in your flesh.—A third point in the arraignment is now brought forward: They do not themselves keep the law. Their zeal expends itself chiefly upon an outward rite. How shallow, after all, is their zeal for the law. It is a zeal which seizes upon an external ritualistic feature of the law and is indifferent to its great moral truths and requirements. The "circumcised" (there is a suggestion of contempt in the term), judged by the standard of real devotion to the law, would make a very sorry showing. Keeping the law in a true and deep sense is quite out of the scope of their purpose.

The fourth element in the indictment is, that their real wish is to glory in your flesh. They wish to persuade the Christians that it is necessary for them to be circumcised, and to have them become so, in order that they may, by this apparent zeal for the Jewish religion, gain favor with the Jews and thus secure themselves against opposition from the Jews. Paul by again using the word "flesh" reminds his readers that all that the Judaizers are doing is done in the sphere of the outward, which by itself can have no spiritual value. Their glorying rests upon that which, in itself, is morally insignificant, and in the spirit in which it is done, is morally reprehensible.

14. But far be it from me to glory, save in the cross of our Lord Jesus Christ, through which the world hath been crucified unto me, and I unto the world.— The opposing position of the Apostle is now defined. He will glory in precisely what they wish to shun, the doctrine of the cross,—that which is the stumbling-block to the Jews; in salvation by Christ through his sacrifice; salvation by God's grace to be received by faith, as opposed to all ideas of salvation by outward deeds or meritorious services wrought by man. For Paul the cross is the symbol of God's love, pity and condescension, the sign and proof of his grace and self-sacrifice. It represents a widely different realm of ideas from those involved in the Pharisaic conception of salvation. Through the cross the world is crucified unto him and he unto the world. The use of the cross as a symbol gives the motive for the figure of crucifixion as applied to the sundering of relations between the soul and the world (κόσμος), this mere outward and transient sphere of things. The cross is the symbol of spiritual and eternal things, God's love, pity and sacrifice. When one apprehends these, they lift him above the world of form and unreality, and sunder his relations to them as by a violent death, *i. e.* "crucify him" to the world. (Compare the relation of the Christian to the law (νόμος): Rom. vii. 4). I refer the phrase **through which** (δι οὗ) to the *cross* (with R. V., Lightfoot; versus Ellicott, Meyer, *et al.*) because, in the connection, **the cross** (σταυρῷ) appears to be the emphatic word, and moreover, the cross is the instrument (διά) of crucifixion. The cross (not Christ as such,—Χριστός = Messiah) is that at which the Jew stumbles and which occasions persecution for the Judaizer; but it is that in which Paul glories, just because it is the means whereby he is liberated from the world of external form, to which circumcision belongs, and brought into the sphere of the spiritual and eternal.

15. For neither is circumcision anything, nor uncircumcision, but a new creature.—By this assertion he illustrates and confirms the statement that by the cross the world is crucified unto him. He, in effect, says: "From my present standing-point, I lay no stress at all upon such outward rites. The only important question is: whether a man is a new creature in heart and life. I care no longer for the outward, these extra-moral observances and relations which belong to the "world;" I am wholly concerned for the inward and spiritual as related to salvation. The fact that I lay the main emphasis upon moral and spiritual character, proves that the world and I have parted company." It should be remembered that the Apostle is here speaking of the attainment of salvation, and is not in any ascetic way expressing contempt for all the relations and interests of the ordinary outward world.

16. And as many as shall walk by this rule, peace be upon them, and mercy, and upon the Israel of God.—The **rule** or canon (κανών) spoken of, is the principle laid down in verse 15. As many as adopt this principle, that newness of life is the all-important thing and not outward conformities regardless of the spirit which is cherished in their observance, peace be upon such **and upon the Israel of God;** an explanatory repetition, as if we said: "Such are the *true* Israel."

17. From henceforth let no man trouble me: for I bear branded on my body the marks of Jesus:—From henceforth (τοῦ λοιποῦ), lit. "during the rest of the time" (genitive of time), that is, hereafter. "Let these hostile annoyances forever cease. Give these false teachers henceforth no place. They are acting a selfish part; but I appeal to my sufferings for the gospel. I bear the marks of the Lord Jesus, the scars and traces of ill-treatment which mark me as Christ's servant and Apostle." In II. Cor. xi. 23 *seq*. he appeals to his sufferings in proof of his full equality with the Judeo-Christian teachers at Corinth. These marks of his devotion to his work and his doctrine he contrasts with the prudential efforts of the Judaizers to avoid persecution. **I bear** (βαστάζω) is said with reference to the dignity and honor which the "brands" (τὰ στίγματα) impart. Such are the credentials of his apostleship and his commendation to their confidence.

18. The grace of our Lord Jesus Christ be with your spirit, brethren. Amen.— The addition of the word **brethren** to the benediction is noticeable in connection with the absence of commendation in the exordium and the severe tone of the letter. He thus closes with an appellation of affection.

APPENDIX.

AN OUTLINE PLAN FOR THE STUDY OF THE EPISTLE.

I. PRELIMINARY STUDIES.

1. READ the entire Epistle with a view to dividing it into its *three* natural divisions, (a) *apologetic*, in which the Apostle defends himself and his teaching, (b) *doctrinal*, in which he explains and defends "his gospel," (c) *practical* or *hortatory*, in which he warns his readers against a possible abuse of his principles and adds exhortations regarding the Christian life.

2. Determine by this reading (or still better, by a *second* reading), (a) what were the personal objections or accusations against the Apostle and his course of life, which had developed in the Galatian churches; (b) what were the grave doctrinal errors in which these accusations had their root.

3. Ascertain from the Acts, (a) what can be known of Paul's visits to Galatia and of his relation to the churches there; (b) seek in the Acts (*cf.* especially xv. 1 with Gal. ii. 12) any light that may be thrown upon the origin, opinions and spirit of the "false

brethren" (Gal. ii. 4) who were stirring up strife in Galatia.

4. In the light of the foregoing studies, define accurately (a) the *occasion*, (b) the *object* of the Epistle.

II. CLOSER ANALYSIS OF THE EPISTLE.

Taking the *apologetic section*, note (a) the *salutation* and by comparing it with those of other Pauline letters, ascertain its *marked peculiarity* and the significance of this for the whole letter. (b) How does the *polemic* element in Galatians differ from that in Romans? (c) Note *the point* of Ch. I and define the bearing upon it of each section of the chapter (as it is divided in the Rev. Ver.). (d) Determine *the point* of Ch. II. and observe the way in which it is supported by *two* series of facts and arguments.

2. In the *doctrinal portion*, study (a) the use made of the case of Abraham and define carefully the *principle* which is thereby established. (b) Note the relation which the Apostle defines between the *gracious covenant of promise* and the *legal system*. (c) Observe the description of the *preparatory office* of the law in leading men to Christ; (d) the way in which Paul illustrates the difference between *freedom* under the gospel and *bondage* under the law. (e) Note his polemic against circumcision and account for it in the circumstances which called forth the Epistle.

3. In the *practical portion* collate (a) the *warnings* against dangers to which the readers were especially exposed, and (b) the *maxims* or *principles* for the Christian life.

III. EXEGESIS.

1. When the Epistle has been thus analyzed and distributed into sections or topical divisions, a more critical study should be made of each part. (a) The writing of a *paraphrase* of a given section is a useful exercise. (b) Each obscure expression should receive careful attention. (c) The rapid rush of Paul's passionate thought in the Epistle has occasioned many grammatical ellipses; the omitted or implied thought should be supplied by a study of the context. (d) In the doctrinal portion, study closely the characteristic *gospel principles* as opposed to the *legal principles,* determining thus the essential content of *Paul's gospel.* (e) Define carefully the relation between the *proto-gospel* ("covenant" or "promise") given to Abraham and the *legal system;* how is this original gospel related to Christianity, and what does this relation prove respecting the relation of *the law* to the *gospel of Christ?*

2. Study with special care the terms which represent the *key-thoughts* of the Epistle, such as *"gospel"* (its origin and content), *"revelation"* (i. 12, 16, when experienced?), *"the gospel of the circumcision"* (ii. 7, how different from Paul's "gospel?") *"pil-*

lars" (ii. 9, why so called?), "*dissimulation*" (ii. 13, Gk: "hypocrisy;" meaning and nature of?), "*no flesh justified by law*" (ii. 16 et al., why? cf. esp. Rom. viii. 3), "*crucified with Christ*" (ii. 20, meaning and origin of this and kindred expressions; collate the passages from Gal. and other Eps. of Paul), "*reckoned for righteousness*" (what is reckoned, why, and how?), "*covenant*," "*promise*," "*mediator*," "*kept in ward*," "*tutor unto Christ*," "*heir and bond-servant*," "*rudiments of the world*," "*weak and beggarly rudiments*," "*fallen away from grace*," "*freedom*," "*walk by the Spirit*," "*the flesh*" (works of), "*new creature*."

3. Certain passages, of special difficulty or importance, may be selected for more exhaustive study, such as iii. 16; iii. 20 and iv. 24–31 (the three most difficult passages in the Epistle). (a) Collate from the foregoing exposition and from other commentaries the leading interpretations. (b) Carefully note the difficulties connected with each. (c) By study of the passage and comparison of views try to elaborate an opinion which shall be *your own*.

IV. BIBLICAL THEOLOGY OF THE EPISTLE.

[REMARK.—A few subjects are here given upon which it is thought that the studies outlined above would enable the student to form intelligent and comprehensive views.]

1. The teacning of the Epistle respecting the *purpose of the law*. (a) The *origin* of the law. (b)

The *mode* of its promulgation. (c) The *time* of its publication as related to the gracious promise. (d) Its *supplementary character* in its relation to the "proto-gospel." (e) Reasons why it *cannot justify*. (f) Its relation to sin; in what sense does it *increase* sin? (g) How can this aim of the law be harmonized with the common view that it was given to *check* transgressions? Does Paul recognize this latter purpose? (h) How does the law by *rousing the power of sin* lead to Christ? (i) Is the law abrogated by Christianity? If so, in what sense? (j) Is it a direct prescriptive authority for the church and the Christian to-day?

2. Teaching respecting *redemption* from the curse of the law by the cross of Christ. (a) What is the "curse of the law?" (b) What does the "cross" mean or symbolize for Paul? (c) How was Christ "made a curse for us?" (d) On what grounds, then, will Paul "glory" only in the cross?

V. SPECIAL TOPICS.

1. Critical comparison of Gal. I and II with the corresponding narratives in the Acts with a view to exhibiting their similarities and differences.

2. Paul's use of allegory in the Epistle and other alleged uses by him of "Rabbinic exegesis."

3. A comparison of the doctrinal method and content of Galatians with those of Romans.

4. A comparison of the Galatian heresies with

those which existed in the church at Colossae with a view to showing in what different ways they threatened the integrity of the gospel.

5. The Apostle Paul as the champion of a universal gospel, including an examination of the nature and extent of his difference from the "pillar" Apostles.

6. Paul's Doctrine of the Christian life as developed in Galatians.

7. Are the law and the gospel, in Paul's view, antagonistic and exclusive of each other; if not, may they become so and under what circumstances do they in fact become so?

8. The use of the Old Testament in the Epistle.

www.ingramcontent.com/pod-product-compliance
Lightning Source LLC
Chambersburg PA
CBHW070247230426
43664CB00014B/2428